Burnout

Burnout:
Stress in the ministry

The Rev Dr John Davey, C. Psychol.,
AFBPsS., FRSH

Gracewing.

First published in 1995

Gracewing
Fowler Wright Books
2 Southern Avenue, Leominster
Herefordshire HR6 0QF

Gracewing books are distributed

In New Zealand by
Catholic Supplies Ltd
80 Adelaide Road
Wellington
New Zealand

In Australia by
Charles Paine Pty Ltd
8 Ferris Street
North Parramatta
NSW 2151 Australia

In USA by
Morehouse Publishing
PO Box 1321
Harrisburg
PA 17105 USA

In Canada by
Meakin and Associates
Unit 17, 81 Aurega Drive
Nepean, Ontario
KZE 7Y5, Canada

Cover design by Rafi Mohammed

Typeset by Action Typesetting Limited, Gloucester
Printed by Progressive Printing, Leigh-on-Sea, Essex

ISBN 0 95244 339 0

Contents

Introduction

Few would doubt that Stress is an intrinsic part of modern life. Without stress we would be unable to experience the thrills and excitement of living. It is the spur which enables us to work harder for longer, and to play harder too. Without stimulation we become dull and depressed, but too much pressure can lead to panic, anxiety, and ill-health. When Stress is excessive, or maintained at a high level for too long a period, the body's natural adaptive powers can fail and the result of such a failure can be personality changes, health problems, and even death.

Both the external and internal events to which the body reacts and to which it must respond constitute stress. The stimuli to set up a stress reaction need not be earth shattering. Stress can arise out of normal, everyday, (insignificant) occurrences just as easily as from major events. Stress has a cumulative effect and minor problems can exert a considerable strain over the course of the day involving a large expenditure of nervous energy. Let me give you an example of what I mean.

I first met Patrick at a deanery chapter meeting. He had expressed a personal interest in the subject I had been asked to talk on. 'I dabble a bit in psychology myself, you know' he said to me. Patrick went on to tell me of his course on psycho-analysis at the local College of Further Education, and of how he used the insights he had gained on the course to counsel his parishioners. I must admit that when he told me this, my heart sank. Not because of his enthusiasm for what I had just said in my talk – we are all susceptible to flattery – but rather because I was concerned about the way in which he had interpreted my observations on psychology and its place in pastoral ministry.

As a priest I believe that Jesus was himself far more concerned with present realities and present solutions than with psychology. So if we accept that Stress plays a big part in our lives, can we also agree on its causes ?

'Arise, take up thy bed and walk', has a painfully practical directness which appeals to me far more than any amount of psycho-analytical questions of the 'tell me about your childhood variety?' As both priest and psychologist I believe that our conscious and unconscious reactions to the challenges and pressures of life – what we do and why we do it – are not just related to the past, but are equally products of the present and future. Knowing who we are, and what we want to be, is the most important ingredient in ensuring our health and well-being.

Many theories have been put forward in recent years, to explain how stress is caused and how we react to it. The earliest of these (Hooke's Law) states that if the strain produced by a given stress falls within the 'elastic limit' of the material, then when the stress is removed, the material will simply return to its original condition. You can test this theory for yourself by thinking back to a time when you have been worried about something and your anxiety has later proved to be groundless; the sense of relief and euphoria can be overwhelming; like waking up from a bad dream and realising that none of what you have experienced was real. If, however, the strain passes beyond this 'elastic limit' then permanent damage can result. Stress can only be tolerated up to a certain point; beyond that point , psychological and physiological harm may ensue. I have never found Hooke's argument entirely convincing. For a start it does not seem to me to take sufficient account of an individual's own level of tolerance, and seems to view stress as a set of causes, and not as a set of symptoms.

Concentrating on the physiological and emotional manifestations of stress (headaches, muscular tension, stomach upsets, tiredness, panic attacks, rapid heartbeat, sleeplessness, and so forth) is also unsatisfactory as it addresses symptoms rather than causes. Psychologists tend to concentrate on the underlying pressures (stressors) which relate to the way in which we live our lives and the work that we do.

Patrick caught my attention again as I gathered up the spare handouts left on the table. 'Have you a spare moment?', he asked. When I said yes I could see that I had thrown him off-balance, and after he had made clear in a nervous voice that he hadn't meant straight away I took out my diary and made a date to see him the following week. Patrick preferred to see me at my home rather than his (though it meant a fairly long drive for him). 'It will do me good to get out a bit, away from the parish' he said. I left his remark unchallenged, and squeezed his arm in farewell as I left the hall.

When the day for the meeting came I wasn't quite sure what to expect. Looking out from my study window I caught sight of Patrick's car parked just a few hundred yards from the rectory. Clearly he had arrived early and was biding his time before driving in to see me. I thought back to the many times when I had done just the same thing: arriving early for an important meeting – drinking a cup of coffee in a tea shop nearby – wishing I hadn't because I then wanted to visit the 'loo'.

I went down to the kitchen to put the kettle on and lay a tray with mugs and a plate of biscuits. Just as the door bell rang the kettle began to whistle. Perfect timing, I thought to myself. Patrick seemed to welcome the coffee which he took white, with sugar.

Even from the first moments of our meeting, it was clear to me that Patrick seemed a very different man to the person I had seen the previous week. His body language was that of someone who was struggling for control and barely achieving it. The coffee was still hot but Patrick was clutching his mug as though his life depended on it. I felt that I had to do something to make him relax, so I suggested that we take a walk in the garden. 'I take all the credit for it, but really my wife does all the hard work', I said to him, searching desperately for something to say to break the ice. Patrick seemed to welcome the distraction, and followed me out-side still clutching his mug. 'What is your garden like ?', I asked.

'Nothing like this', he replied. 'St.Michael's is in the middle of the town and the vicarage is fairly modern; nothing seems to grow there at all; the soil is too acid, I think'.

At last we had made a start. By the time I steered Patrick back to the study and the coffee I had succeeded in getting him to tell me about St.Michael's.

'It's my first appointment as an incumbent', he said. 'Before that I was a curate at St.Andrew's in the city. When the Bishop offered me the living at St. Michael's, Bernard, the parish priest at St.Andrew's, tried to put me off. 'It's not right for you', Patrick, he said. But my wife Mary wanted to settle down, and neither of us wanted to send our children to the local primary school which had a poor reputation. I thought and prayed about the decision a great deal, and we went to see the churchwardens. Mary was quite taken with the parish. There were shops near-by, and the school which was within walking distance seemed just right for Claire and 'Pip'. The PCC were very keen to have us when they met Mary and I. They wanted a family man, someone with kids and we met the bill. I must say I was a little taken aback when I discovered that the vicarage was 'open house'.

The play group is held there three days a week. 'It's the largest house in the parish, and after all it does belong to us', Elsie, the churchwarden's wife explained (Elsie, I gathered, ran the play group).

'After the Family Eucharist, we have the parish breakfast in the vicarage.....Mary gets annoyed about this'. Patrick paused. I waited a moment before asking if Mary was unhappy about sharing her home with other people. 'We argue a lot about this. I say that God's work has to come first, whatever it costs, but Mary thinks we have a right to our own privacy. She say's that she would not have married me if she had thought that she would never have a home of her own. I feel guilty about this.

Mary carried on nursing when I was a student, and gave up her career when I said that I wanted a family. We had Claire when I was still at Theological College, and 'Pip' shortly after I went to St. Andrew's'. 'How do the children feel about this ?', I asked.

Patrick cut in rapidly, 'that's just it. They cannot understand why they have to share their home and their mummy and daddy with other people. 'Pip' is getting very aggressive about it. He has begun to play up on Sundays as soon as the other children arrive. Claire just goes to her room and refuses to come out. Elsie gets annoyed and asks me why I cannot control my children. What can I do ?'. 'And Mary ?', I asked, Patrick looked away and concentrated his gaze on the garden through the study window. 'Mary has threatened to leave me', he said. 'What can I do ?'

'What can I do ?' is a plea echoed by priests up and down the country who experience the pressures of the ministry upon themselves and those closest to them.

In Patrick's case, a word with the area Bishop or Archdeacon, both of whom are in a position to recommend a change of environment, will no doubt solve the immediate problem at least. In other cases the pressures of ministry, might well over time lead to a psycho-physical reaction which at the very least may effect the person's general health and well- being; if prolonged it may even be life-threatening.

To Patrick, as well as to Bill, Geoffrey, George, and Peter*, whom you will read about later, I dedicate this manual which is the fruit of my personal experiences, both as a parish priest and as a chartered psychologist specialising in ministerial stress.

The stress management strategies I outline in the following pages are directed towards the reduction of stress in parochial ministry, the mitigation of the potential consequences of exposure to stress, and the provision of a supportive ministerial environment. They have helped many people over the years. Used properly they could help you, or some-one you love.

* The names I have used in my case studies are fictitious to prevent identification with real places and people. If my readers should identify themselves with particular scenarios or events this is unintentional. However, the fact that comparisons can be made with personal life experiences gives greater credibility to my intent to address those very issues which are cause and occasion for much distress in parish ministry today.

Chapter One

What is Stress?

THE PHYSIOLOGY OF STRESS

Every event to which we are exposed causes an increase in our need to adapt and to re-establish the norm. What does this mean in practice ? Such essentially different things as cold, heat, sorrow, joy, frustration and fulfilment, can provoke an identical reaction in the body. Stress can rapidly bring about physiological effects – anger can cause a rising blood pressure, fear an overflow of adrenaline which augments pulse rate, and constant worry or anxiety can cause muscular tension. A clear example of this conversion from psychological to physiological effects can be witnessed in the bodily tension of some-one who has become anxious about something. Very soon their internal anxiety is outwardly displayed in nervous movement, and stiff, uncomfortable postures. Psychological tension increases muscular tension which in turn leads to tiredness and fatigue. Everyone only has a limited amount of energy available for dealing with the stresses of the environment. If this is consumed in tension, there is little left for the rest of the day's activities. This is why when we are worried or anxious we very often become prone to colds, sinusitis, sore throats, or whatever else in the way of communicable illness is going the rounds. In truth this is what we mean when we say that we are feeling 'a bit under the weather'. Our tension leads to fatigue which in turn leads to lowered bodily resistance to infection. A vicious circle is set up and the more run down we become, the less able we are to cope with and overcome life's problems and hiccups.

To understand and cope with stress, we need to learn more about how the body reacts to fear or anxiety.

1

Of all the many functions undertaken by the brain the continuing health and survival of the body is the most central. Rational thought, language, and other cognitive activities are all secondary to this need and only emerged much later through the process of evolution. When it comes under threat from an external event the brain automatically activates a number of procedures to cope with the perceived danger. These procedures are part of our in-built survival system and are vital to our continued well-being.

In order to understand a bit more about the way these systems work, we should perhaps think a little about what the brain is actually like.

There is an archaeology as well as an architecture to the brain. The oldest and deepest part of the brain is the brain stem, an area which is mainly concerned with the fundamental biological stability of the organism. It manages the primary and most fundamental means of life support, such as the control of breathing and heart rate. The brain stem also acts as an early warning post in processing sensory inputs which might herald the approach of predators or prey.

Sitting immediately on top of the brain stem is the limbic system, a group of cell structures which maintain a stable environment within the body by regulating such functions as the maintenance of body temperature, blood pressure, heart rate, and blood sugar levels. The limbic system does more than just control recurrent internal processes. It can also respond rapidly to a perceived threat by initiating survival strategies which prepare the body for self protection by increasing our ability to stand our ground or retreat.

The limbic system contains the **hypothalamus** – the brain of the brain and its most intricate structure which regulates eating, drinking, sleeping, waking, body temperature, hormone balances, heart rate, and much more. The hypothalamus operates through feedback, for example body temperature is registered in specialised cells in the hypothalamus which respond to the temperature of incoming blood as it circulates through the brain. If the blood is too cool, the hypothalamus stimulates heat production and conservation.

The hypothalamus interacts with the **pituitary** (fig.1). This gland regulates the body through hormones (a word which is derived from a Greek root meaning to activate) which are carried through the blood as chemical messages to specific cells in the body. The pituitary synthesises most of the hormones used by the brain to communicate with the other specialised glands in the body collectively called the endocrine system.

The endocrine or ductless glands, are glands of internal secretion which discharge hormones directly into the blood

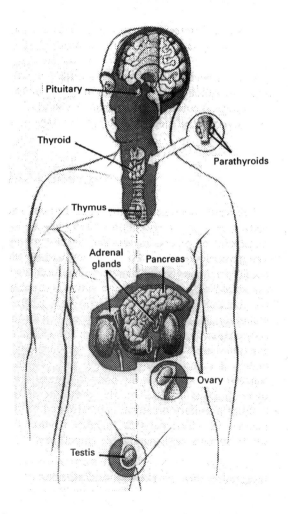

Figure 1

stream, affecting growth, behaviour, and personality (These glands are distinguished from the duct glands, such as tear glands or salivary glands, which secrete their products on the surface of the body or into the body cavities, but not into the blood stream).

There are seven endocrine glands, several of which occur in pairs:

1. The thyroid, which controls metabolic rate, hence activity and fatigue, and body weight;
2. The thymus, which regulates the lymthoid system, and the development of the immune reactions of the body;
3. The parathyroid, which activates and regulates calcium metabolism and the maintenance of normal excitability of the nervous system (arousal levels);
4. The pancreas, which, via insulin, controls sugar metabolism (excess insulin leads to a state of shock);
5. Gonads (testes or ovaries), which maintain the functional condition in the male and female reproductive organs;
6. The adrenal glands, which have two major parts, each secreting its own hormones. The medulla secretes adrenalin and noradrenalin; and the cortex of the gland which secretes a number of hormonal products collectively called adrenocortical hormones.

In the study of the physiology of stress, although other glands may also play a part, the adrenal glands (fig.2) are of particular importance.

The adrenal medulla is active in emotion. Secretion of adrenalin produces many of the symptoms found when a person is excited: tremor in the striate muscles increases; smooth muscles relax; the blood distribution of the body changes; blood sugar is released by the liver into the blood stream and a ready supply of energy is made available; blood pressure increases; and blood clots more quickly in the case of injury. The life-maintaining regulators which control salt and carbohydrate metabolism, secreted by the adrenal cortex are known as steroids. The adrenocortical hormones are so important to the maintenance of life that destruction of the adrenal cortex invariably produces death.

Survival situations demand immediate, short-term, and automatic reactions. The brain's survival response to a perceived

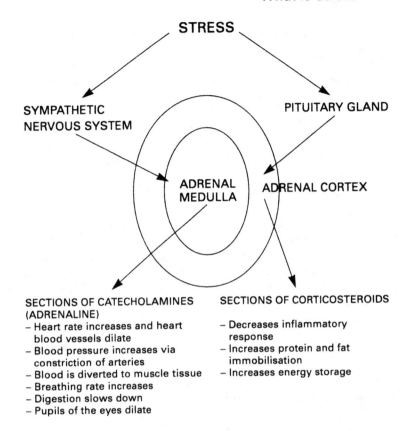

Figure 2 The Adrenal Glands

threat is to activate a complex internal safety strategy. During the alarm phase Catecholamines are poured into the bloodstream causing a number of chemical and physical changes. Blood supply to the muscles is increased through a process of vaso-dilation and vaso-constriction, allowing extra sugar to be carried in case this is needed for fuel during the fight or flight response. In order to do this, the stomach is deprived of blood. If one survives, one can digest food later. The frontal lobes of the cortex of the brain are also deprived of blood which constrains our conscious decision-making.

The cerebral cortex, the latest level of the brain to develop, performs the functions that increase our adaptive ability and is responsible for those characteristics which make us most human. The cortex receives information from the outside world; analyses and compares it with stored information of prior experiences and knowledge, and makes a decision; it then sends messages and instructions to the appropriate muscles, glands and other organs.

It is important to realise that despite our preconceptions the brain as a whole is not primarily designed for thinking. Those attributes which we consider to be most human – language, perception, and intelligence – represent only a small fraction of the functions within the brain which collectively exist to keep us out of trouble.

The brain (not surprisingly) has developed a system to deal with the continuous influx of information which comes into it from the senses and elsewhere. This sorts through the available data and separates the things which can be put on 'hold' from the things which must be dealt with immediately. This priority system gives certain events – in particular those affecting survival – fast access.

Physical Manifestations of stress.

The body responds to any perceived threat by using responses which were originally designed to cope with physical danger. Although it is no longer necessary in our more civilised world for us to respond to all fear-inducing situations in this physical way, our physical reactions have not caught up with our increased intellectual activity and our fear reactions continue to be evoked in an unselective way by a perceived threat to our safety.

EXTERNAL MANIFESTATIONS OF STRESS

1. The pupils of the eyes will dilate. More light will enter so that potential sources of danger may be observed earlier and clearer.
2. Hearing becomes more acute. Danger can be detected at an earlier stage
3. Breathing becomes faster. This increases the amount of oxygen in the blood stream, which acts as fuel for action.
4. The Heart will pump faster and harder so that the flow of fuel is speeded up, and waste products caused by the

increasing rate of fuel burn are carried away quickly.
5. Draining of blood from the exterior so that bleeding will be reduced if the subject is wounded. Another agent ensures that the blood will clot faster, reducing blood loss.
6. Nausea or bowel discomfort may be experienced. This is due to the removal of blood from the digestive system. Vomiting or diarrhoea in extreme circumstances will reduce surplus weight in a flight response.
7. The fuel-rich blood is carried to those muscles which may be needed quickly to aid escape or to fight an antagonist.
8. Sweating reduces heat generated by physical effort by evaporating fluids from the surface of the skin.
9. Shaking or trembling is caused by muscle tension. An additional function of shaking or trembling in the absence of sweating caused by physical effort, is to generate warmth.

These changes are all normal and healthy, and are aimed at ensuring human survival.

THE EFFECTS OF STRESS

Listed below are some of the typical effects of stress or strain. Whilst all these conditions are commonly found in stress victims, they may have causes other than stress or anxiety and it is wise to check first with your doctor to exclude physical conditions.

Feeling low	Sleeping badly	Appetite loss
On Edge	Nightmares	Excessive eating
Irritable	Fainting spells	Need to urinate
Cry easily	Giddy spells	Laugh nervously
Want to run/hide	Trembling	Stuttering
Difficulty in	Sweating	Nervous
concentrating	Breathlessness	Easily Startled
Forgetfulness	Dry mouth	Lacking energy
Putting things off	Lump in throat	Easily tired

MENTAL	EMOTIONAL	BEHAVIORAL
Anxiety	Nervous breakdown	Alcoholism
Depression	Phobias	Smoking more
Feeling helpless	Panic attacks	Addictions
Feeling a failure	Hysteria	Hypochondria
Giving up		

Psychosomatic effects

Some forms of:-

Asthma	Backache	Premenstrual
Hay fever	Neck pain	tension
Allergies	Shoulder pain	Dysmennorhoea
Eczema, rashes	Tinnitus	Impotence
Migraine	Spastic colon	Frigidity
Headaches	Irritable colon	Indigestion
Constipation	Heartburn	Diarrhoea

Physical effects

High blood pressure	Lowered immunity	Chronic pain
Angina	Diabetes	Cancer
Heart disorders.	Arthritis	Peptic ulcer

How to interpret your score

> How to score
> For every tick (✓) in column (a) give a score of 4
> For every tick (✓) in column (b) give a score of 1
> For every tick (✓) in column (c) give a score of 0

If your score is 20 or below you are experiencing the normal stress of life and most of the time responding adequately.

If your score is between 20 and 50 you are experiencing some uncontrolled stress. Most of the time you will appear to others to be coping well. However, you are aware of high stress levels from time to time.

If your score is between 50 and 80 you are probably experiencing most of the symptoms of uncontrolled stress.

If your score is over 80 you might get help from the stress management and stress reduction action plans. However, if you

ESTIMATE YOUR OWN STRESS LEVEL

You can get some indication of your own level of uncontrolled stress by completing the following questionnaire: be as truthful as you can.

You are asked to respond to the following questions by ticking (✓) a, b, or c.

(a) indicates 'most of the time';
(b) indicates 'infrequently';
(c) indicates 'almost never'.

	a	b	c
1. Do you feel irritable for no good reason?			
2. Do you feel that you are building up anger against someone?			
3. Do you feel that other people are against you?			
4. Do you have feelings that you are being neglected?			
5. Do you dislike being physically touched?			
6. Do unfamiliar people or places make you afraid?			
7. Do you feel bad about how you look?			
8. Do you dislike yourself?			
9. Do you have a sense of failure about yourself?			
10. Do you lack confidence in yourself in general?			
11. Do you lack self-confidence in specific areas of your life?			
12. Do you feel disinterested in specific areas of your life?			
13. Do you feel unable to cope with life?			
14. Do you feel trapped?			
15. Do you cry or feel like crying for no good reason?			
16. Do you find it difficult to concentrate?			
17. Do you find it difficult to make decisions?			
18. Do you have dizzy spells for no good reason?			
19. Do you have headaches?			
20. Do you have neck aches?			
21. Do you bite your finger nails?			
22. Do you have unexpected feelings of tiredness?			
23. Do you have problems with sleeping?			
24. Do you fidget?			
25. Do you feel that you need to escape from your life?			
TOTAL			

do not find considerable improvement in how you feel within a period of four weeks **you should seek professional help from your G.P.**

Using the list of Effects of Stress–Strain shown below, circle the number in Questions a-h which best describe your experience in the past twelve months.

EFFECTS OF STRESS – STRAIN

1 = none
2 = very slight
3 = slight
4 = moderate
5 = severe
6 = very severe
I have been experiencing:-

a)	Vague effects of stress	1 2 3 4 5 6
b)	Mental/Emotional/Behavioural effects of stress	1 2 3 4 5 6
c)	Psychosomatic Effects of Stress	1 2 3 4 5 6
d)	Physical Effects of Stress	1 2 3 4 5 6

Months in past year

e)	I have taken tranquillisors for	1 2 3 4 5 6
f)	I have taken sleeping pills for	1 2 3 4 5 6

Times in past year

g)	I have consulted my doctor for effects of stress	1 2 3 4 5 6
h)	I have seen a specialist for Effects of Stress	1 2 3 4 5 6

If you have scored 4, 5 or 6, for a number of the above and there is no physical cause, you may be suffering from quite severe effects of stress or strain.

Scores in the mid-range, especially in Questions a-d suggest mild to moderate degrees of stress or strain.

Ideally you should be scoring consistently at the low end of the scale.

High Scorers –

DO NOT WORRY –
You can improve your score and more importantly your ability

to cope with the stresses and strains of life by adopting a positive action-based approach to your work and life-style.

Low Scorers –

GOOD -
You can keep in the low scores without fear of stress if you maintain your present coping strategies.

Helping others –

You can help others deal with the Effects of Stress-Strain by encouraging them to adopt a more positive outlook on life and, where necessary, alter their present life-style.

PREDISPOSITION TO STRESS

Why is it that some individuals bear stress better than others?

It is a fact that even when faced with the most frightful calamities some people, in spite of the near collapse of their personal world, do not crack under the strain; these people have the ability to pick themselves up by their boot-laces and soldier on. Others experience stress and may become psychologically ill in the face of comparatively minor problems such as a harsh word or gesture from a colleague. How can this be? The answer lies in the inner resources of the person experiencing stress. These resources are just as important to how we cope with stress as the intensity of the stress arising factor. Given sufficient stress, most of us will eventually break down psychologically at a certain point, usually in that breaking point of our personality where we are particularly vulnerable. This varies from one individual to another, as does our predisposition to physical disease; some people are forever getting infections of the respiratory tract, while others tend to suffer from bowel complaints, a cold will go to one person's chest, and to another's sinuses, and so on.

One commonly held view amongst psychologists is that these psychological weak spots are usually determined by influences that make their appearance early on in our childhood, in particular, those which arise from early emotional relationships. In general, those who have felt truly wanted and loved as a child have the best protection and the highest immunity levels from the worst effects of stress. Clearly whatever else may change, certain basic experiences of life such as acceptance, being wanted, valued, and loved, do not. On the other hand certain experiences in childhood such as having unyielding, unsympathetic and over-critical parents or teachers, who withheld due praise for achievements, will tend to make us less sure of ourselves and thus less able to cope with the stresses and strains of life.

PERSONAL CRISIS AND LIFE EVENTS

How often does a stressful incident lead to a heart attack and how often to a cold? Fortunately, the latter is more often the case than the former. There is sufficient evidence to substantiate the belief that stressful life events can and often do act as a trigger for the onset of psychophysical illness of varying degrees of debilitation. However, we should remember that most people do not become severely psychologically disabled when things happen to them, and that for the most part those who do regain their equilibrium in a relatively short time. In truth most of us have the capacity to bounce back fairly quickly after being bowled over by a setback or disaster.

We are constantly faced with situations which require a response of one kind or another. Problems we encounter in our daily lives demand problem-solving activity. In the normal course of events the internal disequilibrium or tension caused by the problem is reduced quickly by solving it through the application of familiar strategies. A crisis only occurs when the usual problem-solving skills are blocked or ineffective, allowing the tension to become out of hand. The tension usually occurs when the person is deprived of some bodily or psychological need.

There are four characteristic phases in the development of a personal crisis:

1. The problem – the stressor – causes tension in the organism which mobilises our usual problem-solving responses.
2. Should these responses, and the problem or unmet need continue to generate feelings of anxiety, guilt, and a sense of helplessness, the person will be unable to function without some degree of disorganisation.

3. When the tension generated by the seemingly insoluble problem passes a given threshold, it becomes a powerful stimulus to the mobilisation of additional crisis-meeting resources.
4. If the problem is not resolved the tension of the unmet need continues to mount until it reaches another threshold. It is at this breaking point that illness is likely to occur.

In psychology, and indeed in life, there are two categories of crisis, developmental and accidental. Human growth is the result of meeting a series of crises successfully. Developmental crises are perfectly normal in the sense that they happen as an integral part of the ongoing transition to maturity. Among these crises are birth, weaning, toilet training, going to school, choosing a vocation, leaving home, engagement, marriage, parenthood, middle age crisis, loss of parents, menopause, retirement, death of spouse, death of friends, and, eventually coming to terms with one's own mortality. These experiences occasion a crisis for an individual to the extent that they pose problems for which previous coping abilities are inadequate.

Accidental crises, as the name suggests, are somewhat different in the sense that they are precipitated by an abnormal and usually unexpected loss of what one believes to be essential sources of need satisfaction. Experiences that can precipitate an accidental crisis include loss of one's job, savings, supportive person, position, status, respect; an incapacitating accident, illness or surgical operation, death of child, marital infidelity and divorce, a physical handicap, an unwanted pregnancy, moving from a place where one feels secure, a natural disaster, or a social calamity such as war or economic recession. These events produce emotionally hazardous situations to which people respond in a variety of ways.

LIFE EVENTS AND THE ONSET OF ILLNESS

There is clinical evidence to support the view that those who looked back at the onset of their illness and had related it to a life event, had in general perceived their environment as more threatening, demanding, and frustrating than those who did not.

Even though life events can and often do cause stress, they

do not do so on their own, for they always operate alongside the more structured aspects of daily living. Life events impact on our daily routines and have a knock-on effect which can and often does make demands upon us which cannot be met by our normal coping abilities. An accumulation of potentially stressful events may provoke a maladaptive physical response which will lower the body's resistance to disease.

Chapter Two

Why is Ministry Stressful?

INTRODUCTION

The nature of ministry as a vocation – a calling – brings with it an acceptance of a personal and grace-given role and function. Ordination confers not only the right and privilege of administering the sacraments of the Church, but also an indefinable quality of chosenness. This process is especially intense in the Roman Catholic Church where the experience of ordination does not simply involve a public acceptance of a role and function, but is similar in many respects to a marriage, mirroring as it does the exchange of vows and promises before witnesses found at a wedding. Ordination makes manifest a person's inner conviction of calling through a commitment to service, which is itself highly dependent on external expression within an organisational context.

Three distinct interaction processes can be identified in the acceptance of the ministerial role. These are Compliance, Identification, and Internalisation.

Compliance occurs when an individual is influenced by external expectations; the priest says or does the expected thing in the performance of the ministerial role. The external role is an expression of compliance which is reinforced by an inner conviction, an underlying faith and a personal belief.

Identification occurs when an individual adopts behaviour derived from a mature concept of the ministry because this behaviour is personally satisfying and rewarding.

Identification serves to maintain the priest's relationship to the parish or form of ministry in which the personal role identification is anchored. Identification differs from compliance according to the degree of personal commitment to the gospel which is proclaimed.

The role is accepted both privately and publicly, and its manifestation is not dependent on the controlling influence of the Church or parish.

Internalisation occurs when an individual accepts the role of priesthood because the role behaviour is congruent with a personally held value system. It becomes part of a personal system, as distinct from a system of social-role expectations. Gradually such behaviour becomes independent of the external source, and it's manifestation is no longer dependent on its being observed by the influencing agent, that is, the Church or the parish, or on the activation of the relevant role. Rather it is now predicated upon the extent to which the underlying values have been made personally relevant.

THE MINISTERIAL ROLE

The role and function of the incumbent has changed radically over the past three decades, both in terms of their status within the community, and in the scope and breadth of pastoral oversight. Former areas of pastoral concern in health, education, housing and employment, traditionally identified with the work and mission of the Church, have been eroded by government agencies and voluntary secular organisations, and the role of the minister redefined.

Ministry today is exercised within the context of a multicultural permissive society which is highly mobile, and which has high unemployment, and an unequal distribution of wealth. It is also a society which has to all intents ceased to recognise the place and purpose of the church in its life.

Lau (1995)* makes the point that when institutions and the norms and belief systems that support them, evolve in an attempt to accommodate rapid social change, this can and frequently does leave those within the organisation in a role

*Lau,B.W.K. (1995) Psychosocial context of stress in health and illness.
J. Royal Society of Health. August 1995.

vacuum in which their internalised values, goals, and aspirations are compromised.

As a condition of living, change can and all too easily does leave those it affects feeling that they have lost control over their destinies. It can undermine their ability to predict the future, and can erode the precepts by which they interpret and derive meaning from experience. It may also engender a profound feeling of loss of the past, leaving them in a state akin to bereavement.

ROLE EXPECTATIONS

Rural Ministry

In England there are 9000 villages with a population of less than 500 people, and many of these villages contain ancient historic churches, the maintenance of which leads at the most to a 'care-taking' and 'conservation' attitude to the local church within the community, and at the least a real fear that it has become too much of a liability and a drain upon community resources.

The Church maintains a presence of a kind in the countryside, but this is a mere shadow of what it used to be within the living memory of many country people. In many places it may amount to no more than a monthly service and a share in a priest who lives some miles away. Pastoral reorganisation has led to the formation of multi-parish rural benefices and it is not uncommon for there to be as many as ten churches served by one incumbent. Fewer clergy are prepared to take on such benefices and a real man-power crisis faces the Church in rural England. It is not unusual for rural benefices to remain without a priest for anything up to two years on the retirement or resignation of an incumbent.

In rural communities village schools, shops and post offices are closing, and public services, especially transport, are being progressively withdrawn.

In many areas a process of population substitution has been in progress for some while, whereby local people move out because of poor housing, limited employment, poor education, poor health and low incomes, to be replaced by commuters, week-end and occasional residents and an ever-increasing army of retired people, who though they live in the countryside, retain an urban life-style, and thus make few demands on local services, which consequentially decline. In the past there has been a tendency to see the countryside as a prosperous and relatively affluent area and to underestimate or even deny the existence of rural deprivation. A disturbing statistic of the present time is the increasing ratio of suicides in the countryside, especially amongst those who are economically dependent on the land.

The second Hereford Rural Consultation in 1986 on 'The People, The Land and the Church', provided that most quintessential of rural dioceses with a basis for thinking about future patterns of ministry. The definition of ministry adopted by the consultation was the church's role: its function, task, and purpose.

Particular patterns of ministry were seen to evolve from different cultural, historical and political periods as a response to need. In this the diocese was acknowledging the need for adaptability in response to external and internal pressure. The flavour of the consultation is encapsulated in its policy statement: – 'Patterns of ministry... must arise from the context of life as it is lived in the here and now....What is absolutely clear from the voices we have heard is that the patterns of the past will not suffice for the future'.

The report stated that the vast majority of people perceived the Church as rich, powerful and hypocritical – sometimes a sham and sometimes an enemy. In such a situation, tinkering with the edges of the structure will achieve nothing.

Perceptions of the Church fell into three categories; namely:-

(1) Contradictions:

The Contradictions reveal that the Church can 'flog itself to death on moral, political and social issues. It can devise pastoral strategy after pastoral strategy, but if it fails to respond, however long it takes, to that most fundamental criticism of its perceived attitudes, options and orientations, then its works will be in vain for generation after generation'.

Support for this view came from the expressed opinion that:-

'They'll have to come to terms with whether they want to be spiritual leaders or a high finance company.'

(2) Personal Vulnerability:

The consultation felt that the Church distinguished between people to the point of prejudice. The laity questioned whether priests knew what it was like to be unemployed. As a consequence they considered the church to be too middle class and to offer too comfortable a concept of faith.

'The Church should pay more attention to community. The Church has spent far too much time being concerned with its own affairs rather than the kingdom of God.'

This was the 'raw material' for a wider discussion on relevant styles of ministry. Put simply, says the report, men and women will have to be able to listen, respond with compassion and indignation, and join people in their search for justice, dignity, equality, spiritual growth and theology. A relevant response will have to include a radically new way of being present locally, to local people.

In psychological terms, the consultation findings may be interpreted as an exercise in conciliation and role negotiation, where, to 'get alongside' calls for the personal vulnerability of the priest. 'Public opinion' or the perception of the priest's role in society was identified in the following observations:-

'You've got to have an understanding minister.'

'Years ago the parson was the centre of activities. He helped on the farms. A typical country man. City parsons don't understand country people.'

[N.B. The point was made in the Archbishop of Canterbury's Commission on Rural Areas (1986) that in former years most parsons were born and bred in the country and therefore brought to rural ministry an understanding of the nature of village communities and people. Today the picture is quite different. The overwhelming majority of ordinands come from urban or suburban backgrounds and bring to rural ministry urban assumptions and patterns of ministry.]

'Could the Vicars learn to understand more about farming?'

'The Vicar, whoever (he) is, should make (himself') known, and visit and be one of the community.'

'Far too much concern with paperwork and there is a lack of pastoral work and concern. There is an apparent remoteness about the clergy.'

'There should be no distinction between laity and clergy. Laity and clergy have different roles, but not status.'

(3) Political Power:

The plea from the people of Hereford was that the Church should become more vulnerable and less remote – a suffering Church, called upon to employ its political power, both locally and nationally, as expressed in the following comments:-

'In the interest of right and wrong the Church must make a stand and soon. It would seem almost that the Church comes on the scene too late. It waits, or hesitates and then attempts to shut the door after the horse has bolted.'

'The youngsters want the Church to be involved in politics, either directly or indirectly.'

'The Church could remind employers of their supposed moral honesty.'

'If a layman could see a Church organisation bringing weight to bear on the large companies and individuals to better our society, there would be more people at church.

The Hereford findings are important in the context of stress reduction in the parish, because they epitomise the often conflicting images which people have of ministry, and draw attention to the dichotomy which exists between the role of the Church as a power structure, and the role of ministry exercised by parish priests within the community.

Urban Ministry

Urban ministry is a term which describes both a geographical demarcation between population density areas – the inner cities and the string of urban villages which form a necklace around them – and the social divide between the have's and the have nots in society. Long-term unemployment has created what might be deemed a non-working class whose anticipation of eventual employment is non-existent; additionally, housing redevelopment policies have eroded one of the most important resources against poverty, namely, the natural neighbourliness of extended families living and working close together.

The Archbishop's Commission on Urban Priority Areas was set up in 1983 to 'Examine the strengths, insights, problems and needs of the Church's life and mission in Urban Priority Areas and, as a result, to reflect on the challenges which God may be making to Church and Nation'.

The indicators of deprivation used in defining UPA's were similar to those produced by the Department of the Environment from 1981 Census Data:-

1. Unemployment
2. Old people living alone
3. Single-parent families
4. Ethnicity: proportion in households with New Commonwealth or Pakistan-born head
5. Overcrowding of homes
6. Homes lacking basic amenities

Urban Priority Areas shelter a disproportionate number of vulnerable people – the unemployed, the unskilled, the uneducated, the sick, the old, and the disadvantaged minority ethnic groups. They are places which suffer conspicuously from low income, dependence on state bureaucracies and social security, ill-health, crime, family breakdown and homelessness. The mission statement of the 'Faith in the City' report which emerged from the commission recognised that the Church does not have particular competence or a distinguished record in proposing social reforms; but the Church has a presence in Urban priority Areas, and a responsibility to bring their needs to the attention of the nation.

The report was seen to be an indictment of government

policy relating to areas of social deprivation and received criticism from the Prime Minister and other members of the cabinet. It was accused by some of taking a political stance that was left-wing, and by others it was seen as reactionary.

'Faith in the City (1985) , advocated reform of the Parochial system to enable ecclesiastical boundaries to equate more closely to those of a 'neighbourhood'. People know where their neighbourhood begins and ends – at a main road, a canal, a row of shops. They know all its significant meeting places – Bingo hall, pub, clinic, playground etc. The Archbishop's Commission suggested that concentrating on the importance of neighbourhoods, should lead the Church to consider the following.

(i)   The need to revise parochial boundaries to relate more closely to such neighbourhoods;

(ii) the development of small neighbourhood-based worship centres. This could lead to 'multi-centre' or multi-cellular strategies for the local church, reflecting a commitment to a locality and not simply to a congregation;

(iii) the development of centres, preferably ecumenical, in each neighbourhood (for example in house groups) which reach out in care and concern for the whole life of the neighbourhood and all its people. Small groups for prayer, Bible study, healing, and theological reflection on local issues would be based on them.

The Report recommended the idea of partnership in the ministry with the hope that each parish reviewed – preferably annually – what progress had been made in the sharing of ministry between clergy and laity, and in cooperation with neighbouring Churches and other denominations.

The Commission also affirmed that in order to make the parochial system more effective, it would be necessary to develop a variety of sector ministries. These would minister to people where they work, are educated, pursue their leisure activities and are treated when sick or infirm. Ministry to specific groups – such as young people, the homeless, and drug addicts and their families – was also recognised as both a need and a legitimate area of pastoral concern.

Despite the high hopes engendered by the report the true

reality is that within the space of a decade, the Church has actually withdrawn to a large extent from sector ministry. Its mission has become entrenched within the bounds of financial constraint.

ROLE PERFORMANCE

Whether the priest is enthusiastic, half-hearted, co-operative, or dogmatic and authoritarian, will largely depend upon his or her innate personality. The expectations are uniform and prescribed by the ordinal and canons of the Church as well as by tradition, but the variations that occur as a result of differing personal conceptions, degrees of acceptance, personality traits, and predisposition, will greatly modify the eventual role performance.

The clergy role enables us to abstract certain normal or stereotyped aspects of behaviour from the full repertoire of an individual's actions. It operates in that strategic area where individual behaviour becomes social conduct. In talking about the clergy role we move away from discussing the personal behaviour of an individual minister, and begin instead to go towards a type of behaviour which can be recognised as occurring for the greater part in ministry.

We recognise a role performance by the situation in which it occurs, and by the fact that the priest when performing such a role is recognised as such within the context of the role environment.

The interaction of the priest and the parish constitutes the social relationship, and one might say that the clergy role materialises only in an interaction setting and only during the performance of ministerial functions.

A number of factors indicate appropriate role behaviour; first, the interaction setting, the parish; and secondly, the various cues associated with the role such as stance, expression, characteristic movement, significant acts associated with ritual and worship, dress, and mode of speech, etc.; Even the role name plays a part in indicating behaviour which is appropriate to the the role, in that it is in itself a guide to appropriate behaviour.

PRIMARY ROLE FUNCTION

Within the multi-dimensional spectrum of priestly function is there an identifiable order of priority ? Clergy refer to the Church's ministry as 'pastoral', and surveys of ministerial attitudes have demonstrated the importance of this aspect of their role. Blizzard's (1956)* role sector categorisation identifies six primary functions of ministry. These are:

a)   teacher of the Christian faith;
b)   organiser of church societies and affairs
c)   preacher of the Word of God
d)   administrator of parish business
e)   pastor of the people
f)   Administrator of the sacraments and leader of public worship.

Using Blizzard's role categorisation, Daniel (1967)* carried out research into the attitudes of ninety-six Anglican Clergy in Greater London. He found that:

53% of the clergy regarded 'pastor' as the most important role sector;
17% priest;
8% preacher;
6% teacher;
0% organiser-administrator.

Using broadly similar role sectors, Ransom, Bryman, and Hining (1977)*, were able to re-confirm the dominance of the pastoral role:-

Rank Order	Role Sector
1.	Pastor
2.	Celebrant
3.	Preacher
4.	Counsellor
5.	Leader
6.	Administrator

*Blizzard,S.W. (1956). The Minister's Dilemma, Christian Century.April, 508-509
*Daniel, (1967) 'London Clergymen', unpublished MPhil. thesis. University of London
*Ransom, Bryman, and Hining (1977),Clergy, Ministers and Priests, Routledge & Kegan Paul

Unfortunately all these research projects failed to provide a comparison with lay expectation of the ministerial role, and can not therefore be used as an indicator of possible stress build-up arising out of a shortfall in expectations.

One important consideration in my decision to carry out further research in the area of primary role perception was the rapid pace of change within the Church during the intervening decade since much of this work was done.

The Swanwick Conference in April 1985 at which some 300 clergy and lay people from the Diocese of Gloucester gathered to discuss the themes of Prayer, Shared Ministry, and Mission, presented me with an ideal opportunity to revisit this area. I invited Conference members to indicate on a scale from one to twelve the most (1) to the least important (12) functions of the priest in parochial ministry. The participants were also asked to indicate whether they were lay or clerical.

The twelve functions selected as representing typical aspects of parochial ministry were drawn from the Ordinal and Canons of the Church of England, and related to four distinct subgroups, namely, Sacramental, Teaching, Leadership, and Caring.

The Caring aspect of priesthood came surprisingly low down in the list of priorities and this may well represent an acknowledgement of the secularisation of a traditional role associated with ministry. The Leadership and Administrative role of the priest was also one which did not figure prominently in the top ranking order. Of great significance, however, was the emphasis placed upon the minister's 'Teaching' role and function. Today the priest is identified more and more as a resource person and an enabler within the structure of a secular church; and in the Diocese of Gloucester, experiments in lay pastorate have featured prominently as valid strategies for urban mission and renewal.

From the Tables (1 & 2) which follow, it is clear that there is a high degree of correlation between the lay and ministerial groups, which would seem to indicate that both priest and people thought alike in their interpretation of primary function in parochial ministry.

The participants were drawn from the broadest spectrum of the Church of England and represented all shades of worship and ritual observance, doctrinal emphasis and persuasion.

TABLE ONE
PRIMARY FUNCTION: CLERGY

1. To be a person of Prayer, Meditation and Study.
2. To Preach and Teach the Word of God.
3. To Administer the Sacraments.
4. To Preside at the Eucharist.
5. To Comfort and Counsel.
6. To Engage in Mission, Evangelism and Outreach.
7. To Lead in Worship.
8. To Care for the poor, the sick and the needy.
9. To Visit parishioners in their homes.
10. To Administer and Manage the affairs of the parish.
11. To be actively involved in Community affairs.
12. To Chair Parochial Meetings.

TABLE TWO
PRIMARY FUNCTION: LAITY

1. To Preach and Teach the Word of God
2. To Administer the Sacraments
3. To Preside at the Eucharist
4. To be a person of Prayer, Meditation and Study.
5. To Comfort and Counsel.
6. To Engage in Mission, Evangelism and Outreach
7. To Lead in Worship.
8. To Care for the poor, the sick and needy.
9. To Visit parishioners in their home.
10. To be actively involved in Community affairs.
11. To Administer and Manage the affairs of the parish.
12. To Chair Parochial Meetings.

In terms of 'role' identification there is a clear indication that clergy see themselves as priests within an apostolic tradition, primarily concerned with the administration of the Sacraments and the proclamation of the Word of God.

The innovative reforms which have been introduced in the past twenty years have most immediately affected the norms of ministerial operation. In Rural ministry the amalgamation of parishes and the establishment of benefices based upon population density, has seriously compromised the historic link between the people and their priests. In Urban ministry, the Churches emphasis upon social action in its search for relevance and meaning in a post-christian society runs counter to the primary role of priesthood as it is interpreted by its clergy.

The recently proposed introduction of fixed term appointments and conditions of service, together with the hierarchy's expressed aim to abolish the traditional 'parson's freehold', will increase the pressure on clergy to be adaptable and resilient in the face of change.

When the dominant roles to which people have become accustomed – for example those associated with a profession – are transformed by choice or situational necessity, the transformation process is often traumatic. An example of dominant role transformation is presented by Zurcher (1983)* in his study of 'dissident' priests who had occupied that status for many years, but had increasingly found the situationally defined role expectations associated with priestly status to be unacceptable to them. They became part of a social movement intended to change the Catholic church.

During 1968, 68 of the 484 Catholic priests in the San Antonio (Texas) archdiocese, signed a petition calling for the resignation of the archbishop, protesting at the archbishop's conservative and authoritarian leadership.

By signing the petition, the dissident priests had taken a stand that transformed their clerical role. Former acquiescents had become activists within the church hierarchy.

Events in the 1960's, including the civil rights and antiwar movements, had influenced them to question their customary role as priests in solving contemporary social problems. They decided that the expectation of priestly obedience to church authority, when that authority arbitrarily enforced conservative social policies, was not consistent with their personal inclinations or spiritual obligations. Zurcher found that the potential or actual loss of a dominant role, whether by choice or because of circumstances, causes a person to examine, evaluate, and eventually redefine his or her self-concept.

* Zurcher,L.A. (1983) Social Roles. London: Sage Publications

Responses to the 'WHO AM I?' question posed by Zurcher, were agonisingly reflective and emotionally profound, as illustrated by the following evaluation

Zurcher (1983) Who am I? N = 24

- I am a confused man
- I am frustrated with the Church
- I am lonely
- I am in need of the help and consultation of others
- I am less trusting than I was in past years
- I am worried
- I am unsure of my abilities
- I am re-evaluating my beliefs
- I am becoming more withdrawn
- I am uneasy in my self-image
- I am useless to many people
- I am abrupt sometimes
- I am not very organised

Zurcher's dissidents, having chosen to transform their priestly dominant role, were evaluating not only the new direction that the role might take but also the conceptions of self that had been linked to that role.

The priests in Zurcher's study who had elected to attempt transformations of the dominant roles they had long enacted and which were historically supported by the powerful organisation in which their role was embedded, were not however inclined to leave the church organisation.

The inherent contradictions generated within the Church have been brought to the surface by the pressure for change. Even among those aspects that characterise its clergy as professionals, there are conflicting movements. The clergy are caught up in a series of measures which will radically alter the nature and function of their ministry at the parish level. At risk in the process of change is status, authority, and self-identity.

ROLE CONFLICT. ROLE AMBIGUITY, AND ROLE OVERLOAD

Role conflict, role ambiguity and role overload have long been associated with stress. Within the clerical profession, this is particularly true, because of the close identity between the role and its enactment in a social and organisational context.

Role Conflict   exists when an individual is torn by conflicting work demands, or is asked to do things that he or she does not want to do or does not think are part of the job.

One example of this would be when a person is caught between several groups each of which has differing expectations of what should or should not be done.

Because of the multifarious nature of the ministerial role, the different functions carried out by the minister often vie and conflict with one another. A priest is required to be a teacher, preacher, social worker, evangelist, comforter, sustainer, prophet, peacemaker, administrator, fund raiser; and a youth worker; to be popular, able to fill the church to overflowing, be a Godly example to the community, and available at all hours of day and night to meet the particular needs of parishioners.

Role conflict occurs when the minister's attitudes, values, motives and priorities are at variance with others. Role conflict has been keen to arise from low work satisfaction and high work related tension. The life of a priest is a succession of roles which frequently cause friction and stress. When a minister is also a family person, there is often conflict between the work and family role – a conflict which is cited as the most frequent cause of marital breakdown. Within the clerical role there is often a disparity between expectation and reality. This can be associated with the particularly rigid, moral, ethical, and behavioural mould in which the priest is cast by society. Within the role performance there is opportunity for the expression of a personal identity and individuality.

When individual differences are expressed in terms of behaviour which is outside the norm of social expectation, it is not the role which is compromised so much as the interpersonal relationship between the priest and his or her parish.

Role Ambiguity   exists when an individual has insufficient information about the work role. Several sources of role ambiguity have been identified in ministry – lack of sufficient information about the scope and responsibilities appertaining to ministry; lack of information about the expectations others have of the ministerial role, especially colleagues and parishioners; insufficient feedback, and insufficient preparation for pastoral ministry.

Appointing bodies often assume that leadership skills are present, in spite of the fact that, if it is a first appointment, the prospective incumbent will have had little or no experience in executive decision-making. At present the Church of England does not have a uniform system of practical training for prospective incumbents. In practice therefore training may consist of no more than observing and perpetuating the mistakes of others.

Likewise the expectations which parishioners have of a new incumbent are formed largely as a result of their experience of the previous incumbent and the way in which he or she did things.

By the nature of the calling the priest has a self-defining role and function in society within the parameters of an accepted norm. The role conception will therefore reflect to a large extent individual personality coupled with learning and experience. Unfortunately this self-definition may not correspond to the role expectations of others, and it is within this area of conflicting conceptions and expectation, that many of the problems associated with a breakdown in parochial communications may lie. However, a mismatch between role enactment and role expectation does not necessarily change a potentially supportive environment into a stressful one.

It is a fact that whilst a person may well describe the ambiguity factor in his or her work role as exceedingly high – far greater than expected – he or she may well go on to say but 'This is what really excites me about it – I wouldn't be without it'. In a similar situation, another person may however, say 'It is often daunting. I'm never sure what I am doing, or why. How on earth can I cope with such a situation?'.

Individuals who suffer from role ambiguity have been found to experience low work satisfaction, high work-related tension, and low self-confidence. These problems are mirrored by physical ailments – increased blood pressure and pulse rate, and depression – which can lead to voluntary relinquishment of office, and/or early retirement. Clearly for certain individuals role ambiguity can be an important factor in raising their stress levels.

Role Overload   The priest is rarely if ever off duty. Unlike other professionals there is no clear distinction between the priest's work role and non-work role. The 24 hour nature of a priest's work leads to a number of in-built conflicts which are causes of stress not only for the incumbent, but also for immediate family members. The clergy role is for the greater part indistinguishable from the priest's personal life and this is expressed in terms of time commitment.

Having a 'day off' is viewed by many clergy as an act of truancy.

5% of clergy in rural areas or villages claim that they can never get a day off, often because they are the sole person responsible for the parish. According to the Gallup Survey of 1986* 14% of clergy in rural areas 'do not have an annual holiday of at least two weeks away from the parish',

Having too much to do – quantitative work overload – or being underqualified – qualitative work overload – is now endemic within the clerical profession.

The heavier work load, increased administration and responsibility, duplication of services (especially at Festivals), longer hours, time taken in travelling between widely scattered parishes, and the increased emotional and empathetic commitment, brought about by the decrease in ministerial resourcing, has been reflected in a significant rise in perceived stress among multi-parish benefice clergy.

ROLE STRESS

'Priesthood is acknowledged as a stressful occupation and many of its practitioners exhibit recognisable signs of stress,' writes Hales (1986)*. He adds, 'To be a priest is to live in a potentially pressured and stressful position; some of the pressures are similar to those experienced by other professionals, in similar caring occupations, while others are specific to the nature of the exercise of priestly ministry. These pressures may be related to the demands of the task, either in the general (such as relationships with parishioners, PCC, etc.), or in the specific (such as the stress arising from pastoring the

*Gallup Survey of Church of England Clergymen (1986): General Synod of The Church of England.
*Hales,G. (1986) The Family Man (unpublished)

bereaved); or the pressures may surround factors in the position of the priest in (his) own family, often placed in a fairly public situation'.

Hales summary of the problems experienced by clergy is confirmed by an earlier study undertaken by Eadie in 1973*. Eadie's survey showed that within a sample of 85 clergymen, over 68% of them had experienced psychophysical disorders, neurotic problems, personality difficulties and emotional stress which was of sufficient intensity to require absence from work. This study indicated that ministers of religion were subject to external demands from their parishioners, and frequently lacked support and appreciation for the work they did. The external sources of stress were thought to be far less damaging than the intrapersonal ones – habitual self-criticism verging on self-denigration, low self-esteem, a sense of inferiority and personal dissatisfaction.

There would appear to be a pattern and sequence to the way in which stress develops within those working in the ministry. This pattern has three distinct stages:

1. A shortfall between demands and resources. Stress is experienced when an individual endeavours to meet the demands of too great a work-load by working longer hours, missing meals, giving up leisure time and recreation, and neglecting their family. This pattern is fairly typical of the kinds of situation which have arisen within many Church of England parishes in recent years as a result of the formation of multi-parish benefices and the extension of town parish boundaries. In other parishes qualitative work overload may be the result of the minister being unable to meet the level of ability and confidence required to fulfil the challenges raised by a particular administrative assignment.
2. Without help and support from colleagues and senior clergy, the individual is increasingly unable to cope. This leads to a second stage, which is characterised by feelings of anxiety, anger, tension, fatigue and exhaustion.
3. When matters become chronic, a third stage, is reached in which the minister may experience radical changes of attitude and behaviour.

*Eadie,H.A. (1973). Health of Scottish Clergymen. Contact, 4 (Spring Edition).

CAREER DEVELOPMENT AND MINISTERIAL STRESS

Career Development research has identified three distinct stages which are relevant to stress research. These are: establishment, advancement, and maintenance. Different career stages may emphasise different stressors. In the case of clergy, the initial stage of ministerial establishment after ordination is appointment to a 'title' as an assistant curate.

This period of career development corresponds to the first category above. In the early years, 'relationships' particularly with senior clergy, may be of paramount concern. This will relate to both feelings of security and also provision of information about the organisation and the employee's own performance.

Hughes (1958)* refers to the 'reality shock' associated with the socialisation process when the individual learns and acquires the values and orientations of the organisation. Role ambiguity may be experienced at this stage and early experiences may affect future attitudes, expectations and performance. During the period of advancement, when the offering of a 'living' will involve decisions affecting other family members, the source of stress may well occur at the work-family interface. Preoccupation with the job during advancement years is liable to have a disrupting influence on family life. Relationships within one's family and with colleagues will be crucial at this stage and may well involve a degree of 'bargaining' and the foregoing of personal ambitions and aspirations to further career prospects and future plans – where these conflict with family needs, e.g., children's schooling or employment, and/or a spouse's dual career prospects.

At the maintenance stage of career development, career frustrations, fears of obsolescence, or negative organisational attitudes can come to dominate an individual's concerns. The threat to the continuing existence of the parochial system and the 'parson's freehold', fixed term contracts, pension and retirement housing provision, new forms of ministry, and an ever-increasing level of accountability – both at the diocesan

---

* Hughes, E.C. (1958) Men and their Work. Glen.Ill.

and parish level – also feature as potential stressors at this stage of ministry.

IDENTIFIABLE STRESSORS IN MINISTRY

The objective of the Gallup Survey of 1986 prepared for the Archbishop's commission on Urban Priority areas, was to gain a systematic view of ministry as currently discharged by the Church of England.

Its findings – especially in relation to the problems which clergy face in their ministry – illuminate and draw attention to specific stressors which were perceived to be present in the

TABLE THREE
THE TWENTY MOST WIDESPREAD PROBLEMS
(Gallup 1986)

		Total %
1.	The amount of administration	53
2.	Problems with church buildings	50
3.	Secularisation of the surrounding culture and people	42
4.	Feelings of irrelevance to the church/to the world around	38
5.	The members of the church congregation who come from the parish but do not want to minister to it	34
6.	Failure to find members of the congregation with whom to share leadership/ministry	33
7.	Difficulty of getting away for days off	30
8.	Difficulty of getting away for longer breaks	30
9.	The expectations of non-church people in the local area	29
10.	The expectations of the congregation	28
11.	Lack of defined and achievable objectives	28
12.	Lack of visible results	28
13.	Members of the congregation have different priorities for ministry from your own	28
14.	Sparsety of other full-time ministers serving alongside	22
15.	The small numbers of congregation	22
16.	Exhaustion	20
17.	Personal finance	19
18.	Being helpless in face of injustice suffered by those being ministered to	19
19.	Inappropriateness of training at theological college/ course	18
20.	Lack of ecumenical co-operation	17

TABLE FOUR
CURRENT PROBLEMS IN MINISTRY
(Gallup 1986)

		Total %
1.	Difficult relationships with congregation/ individuals in parish	42
2.	Personal doubts as to the 'worthwhileness of their ministry	29
3.	Personal/Family financial problems	27
4.	Other personal/family problems	27
5.	Difficult relationships with PCC/church officers	25
6.	Caring for elderly parents/relatives	24
7.	Illness (own or family)	22
8.	Difficult relationships with fellow clergy	20
9.	Having to depend on financial help from others	11
10.	Personal problems of faith and belief	11
11.	Having to depend on financial help from parents/parents-in-law	9
12.	None of these difficulties	11

occupational environment. In Addition, according to the survey, clergy perceived particular problems with regard to their ministry in relation to both interpersonal relationships – doubts as to the 'worthiness' of their ministry – and personal problems concerning their families and finances.

In reply to the Gallup Survey question 'in which areas of your ministry, if any, do you feel a lack of support or valuation or management ?', the greatest area of criticism was lack of support from parishioners, and the hierarchy.

The 'Gallup' findings give an indication of the likely sources of stress in ministry. Of particular importance is the picture that it presents of an occupational group who perceive themselves to be overworked, under-supported, under-appreciated, and with a lack of confidence that their particular skills and aptitudes will be recognised and utilised by those in authority.

TABLE FIVE
PERCEIVED LACK OF SUPPORT OR UNDER-VALUATION
(Gallup 1986)

		Total
1.	None	39
2.	From parishioners/officers	16
3.	From hierarchy	12
4.	In administration/secretarial	10
5.	In general parochial ministry	8
6.	Working alone/isolation	4

TABLE SIX
PERCEIVED REAL SUPPORT IN MINISTRY
(Gallup 1986)

	Total %	Married	Single
Wife and family	75	88	9
Church wardens	50	52	44
Individuals in parish	48	48	48
PCC/Church officers	44	45	38
Personal friends	42	39	57
Suffragan Bishop	31	30	37
Archdeacon	29	29	28
Diocesan Bishop	26	26	24
Informal group/neighbouring clergy	24	25	19
Rural Dean	24	24	26
Spiritual Director	22	21	25
Clergy Chapter of Deanery	20	20	17
Mixed group from parish	19	19	19
Group/Team ministry	12	13	7
Ecumenical group	11	11	11
Other clergy	11	10	18
Canon missioner	3	3	0

STRESS AND SOCIAL SUPPORT

It is clear from Table 6 above that most of the social support which clergy receive in the exercising of their ministry comes, not from their Bishop, but from the local environment, especially from their immediate family circle and parishioners.

The social environment of the clergy is not just a major source of stress, it also provides vital resources which the individual can and must draw upon to survive and flourish. The positive effects of social support in preventing, coping effectively with, and recovering from stress related illness, lie in the benefits to be gained from problem sharing and the reduction of uncertainty and worry. However problem sharing – in the case of the clergy – can have a counter-effect upon the health and well-being of a spouse. It is not always the case that 'a problem shared is a problem halved'. Fletcher (1988)* has drawn attention to the similarity in the stress levels of clergy and their significant others which indicates that all too frequently stress acts like a virus which can be passed on to those closest to the source.

The perceived lack of support from professional colleagues and from the church's hierarchy, has the negative effect of creating uncertainty and doubts about self-worth.

In terms of coping, the positive and beneficial effects of social support are related to information-sharing and sympathetic understanding. Where these factors are lacking, the priest may well become resentful, irritable and uncooperative.

A perceived lack of support or under-valuation (Table 5) from parishioners/church officers and from the hierarchy, relates directly to the perceived problems in ministry found in Table 4. This is especially true with regard to difficulties in relationships with congregation/individuals in the parish, and doubts as to whether an individual's ministry is worthwhile.

There are at least two very different ways in which social support might be relevant to coping with stress.

First, there is the assumption based upon a body of research related to attachment and dependence, that being embedded in a social network is essential for people to feel good about themselves and their lives. Viable social relationships make possible identification and involvement. The second assumption is that support acts as an immediate buffer to stress and its destructive and psychophysical consequences. It can also help in stress prevention by making harmful or threatening experiences seem less consequential and can provide valuable resources for coping when stress does occur. The Gallup report of 1986 highlighted the importance of effective support and appreciation from the hierarchy in acting as an effective modifier/buffer to potential stressors in the ministry and concluded that where clergy did not have frequent personal

*Fletcher, B. (1988) Occupational Risk Transmission (unpublished)

talks with someone who had direct pastoral responsibility over them, they were liable to suffer a significant loss of self-esteem.

The former pattern of priests living a communal life and exercising their ministry under the watchful eye of a senior cleric – a situation that was extremely common in the Roman Catholic Church – had many advantages; not least that of being part of a team and the opportunity this provided for mutual support, companionship, and corporate worship. For the most part, such opportunities no longer exist; all too frequently, priests, especially those who are unmarried and who live on their own, feel isolated and marginalised.

The most telling need among clergy today is for guidance and reassurance as to the relevance and meaning, of their intrapersonal and parochial lives. In the past, clergy received their assurance and awareness of self-worth from the nature of their status and role within the community and parish in which they served. Today this is no longer the case and the authority figure, be it the bishop, archdeacon, or rural dean, will increasingly be called upon to act in a supportive capacity as 'Pastor Pastorum'. At the present time the burden of administration appears increasingly to be the main factor in shaping the role played by senior clergy, and the increasing weight of synodical government has meant that too much time is taken up with considerations of diocesan and national importance at the cost of local needs and identity.* A major criticism levelled by parish priests at senior clergy is that all too frequently they are not available for advice and consultation when an emergency occurs in the parish. There is a deep seated reluctance on the part of clergy to accept ministerial appraisal or accountability, which means that there is neither the opportunity to evaluate the effectiveness of an incumbent's pastoral ministry, nor the occasion to give due praise and support where it is merited.

For their part, incumbents have an obligation to serve their parishioners in the best possible way, and senior clergy would wish to facilitate this by providing every opportunity for personal growth and the acquisition of pastoral and interpersonal skills through the provision of a suitable support and

*It is too early to say what effect the changes advocated by the Turnbull report, if implemented, will have on this situations.

training structure. Many of the problems currently facing the clergy may be directly attributed to a lack of support, sympathy, understanding, and appreciation in one form or another. The failure to provide an effective support network for clergy, which would include problem and anxiety sharing between the incumbent, the hierarchy, colleagues, and parishioners, can only lead to an increase in perceived stress and its somatic consequences.

THE HOME/WORK INTERFACE

In 1983 the following headline appeared in the Church of England Newspaper – 'Church to give aid to deserted wives'. Clergy families are no different from other families and are subject to the same degrees of stress with perhaps an added element of stress caused by the nature of the profession.

Sometimes things go terribly wrong and when they do the stress generated is compounded by the feelings of guilt and sense of failure experienced by all parties.

The scale of marital breakdown amongst the clergy has now reached crisis proportions, according to a spokesman for the General Synod.

To quote Pauline Morrell, secretary of 'Broken Rites' (a support group set up in the early 1980's), clergy wives 'feel they are expected to set an example, and that they are letting the Church down as well as jeopardising their husband's careers when they admit defeat. Sometimes it makes them turn their backs on the Church they have loved and served, especially if parishioners have been less than understanding. The obvious difficulty is housing, there being no family home to split and the vicarage being needed for a new incumbent. In most cases there are no savings to divide up and little enough to contribute to maintenance.'

Historically, most parishioners saw the role of the parson's wife as essentially one of support for and active participation in her husband's ministry. This was often accompanied by a tacit assumption that as well as acting as companion, mother and housewife, the clergy wife would also fulfil the office of secretary, 'gofer' and unpaid assistant curate. Hopefully the removal of the exclusively male nature of priestly ministry may do much to change this traditional role.

The incumbent has two problems in meeting the needs of immediate family members; the first is time and commitment management. Not only does the busy life of an incumbent leave little time for the family, but having expended all available emotional resources upon others there is nothing left when it comes to family needs and crises. Secondly, there is the possibility of crises or stresses spilling over from the work environment to the home.

Under normal circumstances, people find their home to be a haven and refuge from a competitive and demanding work environment – a place where they can expect to find support and comfort. However incumbents cannot so easily separate their work from their home. The parsonage is the 'nerve centre' and 'command post' for parish activities which take place outside the church building. The parsonage is the place where the parson is available at all hours. It is the parish office, the consulting room, the confessional, the point of attack and the point of defence, the advance station and the rearguard area for casualties. The clergy spouse shares both battle honours and battle wounds. Criticism and complaint are fired indiscriminately at the visible and vulnerable human face of the Church, the incumbent, and the incumbent's family at home. Another source of stress for many clergy families is the present legal requirement that whilst in office the incumbent lives in the parsonage thereby precluding the possibility of benefiting from the acquisition of property as a form of saving and preparation for retirement. Most clergy cannot afford a second home and find it extremely difficult to save for retirement from their stipend.

A further cause for stress which is also associated with the 'tied' nature of the priest's accommodation, is the fact that if an incumbent dies in office, the parsonage will no longer be available as a home for the family, and an alternative house will need to be found within a period of twelve weeks.

The Faith in the Countryside Report (1990)* drew attention to the particular stressors which pertain to rural ministry and the need for greater support to be given to such clergy and their families. At one level, the report points out, there is little difference between the situation faced by clergy families

*Faith in the Countryside: 1990. Churchman Publishing.

and that faced by other families in the countryside. In most cases clergy families do enjoy a reasonably high standard of accommodation without the worries of maintenance, but at the same time they face the limitations imposed by the lack of services and are protected only by a very modest income. There is also an expectation that the lifestyle of modern-day rural incumbents will mirror that of their predecessors whose income, based on tithe rents and personal wealth, was much higher. To quote the report: 'The predicament can be characterised as a tension between high expectations and limited resources'.

According to the Rural Church Project findings*, 71% of rural churchgoers felt that clergy wives have or should have a supportive role to play in the parish; surprisingly, the survey found that a significant number of clergy themselves were keen to ascribe a role to their wives. To quote from the report:- 'There is less evidence of what is expected of clergy husbands, though one woman deacon told us that she was asked why her husband should join her in the vicarage rather than provide her with a home!'

Evidence suggests that clergy wives in rural parishes may be particularly vulnerable, and that some younger clergy wives were taken by surprise at the level of personal hostility directed against them when their husbands pursued an unpopular course of action.

Clergy wives are frequently called upon to counsel and advise people with problems who want to talk to a woman, yet such counselling – usually undertaken without any form of training – puts a great strain on those who feel unable to respond, or who do not want to be used as an alternative to their husbands. Clergy wives are often treated as being adjuncts by implication to their husband's job, with the same degree of vocational dedication and training in theological and pastoral skills, rather than as people in their own right. It is sometimes assumed that a wife's commitment to her husband and family – which is freely given and which is frequently the major factor in making a difficult job possible, also automatically extends to commitment to the Church. Although this can be said of other clergy situations, the point about rural

*The Rural Church Project: The Centre for Rural Studies, RA College, Cirencester, and the Dept. of Theo. University of Nottingham.

ministry is that in the countryside clergy and their spouses have a much higher profile.

A further observation in the *Faith in the Countryside Report* was that single clergy, particularly men, felt that their sexuality was under question and some gave evidence that they were asked specific questions on their sexuality when being interviewed for a post by parish representatives.

The report found that the clergy chapter was most often cited as providing the best support for clergy by enabling them to meet together for prayer and study. It was a point at which stress could be detected, initiatives considered and morale encouraged. This was especially so for incumbents of multiparish rural benefices.

A recurring theme in the report was the problem of isolation, which can 'be exacerbated by the lack of readily available independent counselling...we recommend that courses to increase self-awareness and group experience are a routine part of inservice training.'

GENDER STRESS

The final report of the 'Windsor Consultations on Women in the Ordained Ministry' (1991), noted a concern for the material, psychological and spiritual welfare of women currently serving as ordained ministers in the Church of England. To quote, 'In psychological terms, women are suffering, sometimes acutely, from the lack of security, direction, development and fulfilment in their ministries'.

In 1992, the author and colleagues from the Department of Occupational Psychology, Birkbeck College, University of London*, conducted a survey of women deacons, prior to their admission to the Priesthood. Much of what follows in this section will be distinctively Anglican, however many of the same issues have already been raised in the independent churches who have appointed women ministers, and may help to inform the current debate taking place in some Roman Catholic Churches. In the sample group as a whole, 60% were University graduates, 10% held higher degrees, 31% held

*Shipley, P. Davey, J., & Orlans, V. (1992) Stress Research & Control Centre, Birkbeck College, Univ. of London.

Certificates in Education, and 18% had dependent children living at home. All had a wide range of experience and competencies which they utilised in their parochial ministry within the broad categories of education, administration, and socially focused roles, but without the full recognition which such duties normally attract where the the role incumbent is male.

Prior to their acceptance into the priesthood of the Church of England, many women took a cynical perspective, playing down their aspirations (and, by definition, their creative energy)., while many others attempted to be realistic and pragmatic.

Individual coping strategies ranged from resigned acceptance ('I am fortunately very realistic'), and rationalisation ('I'm doing as well as can be expected'), to the extreme of just 'hanging in there' ('sometimes I'm nearly swinging from the light bulbs').

With regard the effects of their ministry on their general health and stress, the picture which emerged was a uniform one. Many reported their work to have a beneficial effect on their health; others were less sanguine, and drew upon a range of social supports to help them, including turning to prayer and meditation, and taking time off when stress levels became unmanageable. No less than 57% indicated that their health and well-being had suffered as a direct result of the work that they were doing. The contributory causes cited included:

relationships with colleagues	22%
pressure of work	18%
present/previous occupational environment	17%

There is at the present time no policy of Equal Opportunity within the Church – a fact which has its roots in its historical, cultural and political development, and the issues of Sexism, Gender and Equal Opportunities were reflected in a variety of ways in the above study.

Among the sample of women deacons surveyed, 45% referred specifically to hostility shown towards them, by male colleagues especially, parishioners and members of the public. Even where overt hostility was not shown, they felt it was implicit in the gross under-utilisation of their pastoral, and intellectual skills and experience.

The Church's role as an employer has evolved from its position as a powerful, male-dominated, elitist professional body. This model of male supremacy has persisted into the present day, and is likely also to underpin the over-valuing of the sacramental dimensions in ministry, and the comparative under-valuing of the social and pastoral roles. From such a perspective one could argue that men in the Church could feel threatened by the idea of women taking over a traditional 'male' domain. In addition, there may also be deep seated psychological feelings of threat induced by the prospect of women taking on roles which provided men with an outlet for 'nurturing' needs which have not been condoned so readily in other occupational settings.

Vocational preference research has drawn attention to the relationship between career choice and personality traits, and also to a gender specificity in relation to work orientation; the particular personality traits which are recognised as strengths in ministry are, typically, attributes of caring, compassion, sustaining, and supporting.

Specific issues were identified during the course of the Shipley, Davey, and Orlans (1992) research, which will be of concern to those who are interested in the effectiveness of the Church as an employing organisation.

First there was the question of the effectiveness of pragmatic managerial strategies which may appear to meet a number of immediate needs, but which may have serious implications for future functioning in terms of reducing morale, increasing resentment, and impairing the potential for creative teamwork.

Of particular importance is the view that women priests have been introduced at a time when there is a 'manpower' short-age within the Church, a fall in the number of those who regularly attend Church Services, and a corresponding reduc-tion in Church giving which has been compounded by a cut-back in resourcing from the Church Commissioners.

A second consideration concerns the extent to which women have been invited to collude with a system which is not in support of their shorter or longer-term interests. At present women priests are on a career ladder whose top rungs are not yet in place. Whether or not women wish to go to the top of this ladder is less important than that they should feel free to have the choice to do so if they wish. From a managerial perspective this is an Equal Opportunity question and encompasses issues of value, politics, and managerial strategy.

In the longer term it cannot surely be in the interests of the Church to maintain such a power differential in relation to a group of employees who are likely to form an increasingly important part of the organisation's work-force in the future. An additional consideration is the way in which this situation may impact upon the Church's image amongst the population of an area as a whole.

To make these points is not to enter into the debate over the theological implications of the decision to ordain women as deacons, priests or ministers, but rather to point out what that decision has meant in practice for the women involved.

Stress levels, as indicated by the above survey, were comparatively high, and one could argue that stress is likely to form a significant part of individual and group experience within the Church in its acceptance of women as priests.

If the job roles and well-being of women priests, and their location within the employing organisation of the Church are to be considered, the Church and those in authority within it needs to move towards evaluating the 'masculine' and 'feminine' within the Church, and to begin to ask theological questions relating to the masculinity of God, and the way in which the 'feminine' is traditionally included in Christian teaching – e.g., the virginal innocence of Mary, and the seductiveness of Eve. There is an ambivalence here which can undermine the position of women in the priesthood, and drive other women out of the Church entirely. Having set out on a path of involving women more fully in its life and practice, the Church needs to be prepared to follow its initiative through if it is not to actually increase the pressures felt by women within the Church.

No less ambivalent is the Churches position regarding homosexual priests. According to Fletcher (1989)* one in every seven Church of England clergymen is a homosexual, and many are suffering from abnormal levels of stress because they fear exposure (Fletcher's sample group was drawn mainly from parish priests who were members of homosexual support groups). The survey suggests that seven per cent of homosexual clergy opted for the 'halo of marriage'. A quarter however lived with a same sex partner, despite the Church's stance that 'homosexual genital acts fall short of the Christian ideal.

* Fletcher, B.C. (1989) Clergy Under Stress: Mowbray

There was evidence in Fletcher's findings, that homosexual men are more vulnerable than heterosexuals to stress and stress related substance abuse (alcohol and drugs). The elevated stress levels found within Fletcher's population group have been variously attributed to problems of identity, or failure to find a satisfactory self-image – the gay parson's principal problem becomes one of finding an acceptable identity within a hostile environment.

Fletcher attributes his findings to a constellation of interrelated factors, some internal, some to do with vocation, some to do with external pressures (from the Church and others), and some to do with the normal stresses and strains of life, which in the absence of support and the ability to share these with a 'significant other', become more destructive to health and well-being.

Priests are by definition deeply religious people with particularly caring attitudes. They are judged worthy of their calling by their ability to demonstrate gifts of sensitivity and responsiveness to human need. However, these gifts increase the probability that homosexual priests will be prey to inner doubts about their own worthiness which the Scriptures themselves cannot resolve fully. As Fletcher points out, 'The homosexual clergyman may even question his very faith because for him God has made him homosexual in a heterosexual world. He may question his own morality and his own behaviour. He may be forced into behaviours he is uncomfortable with because of insufficient channels for sexual release. He may question his weakness. He may question his God. He may question his very being'. Heterosexual clergy do not have to face such deep questioning. Priesthood makes special demands upon the homosexual who is expected to uphold and adopt a code of values and ethics within a high profile occupation in the community which may be at variance with his sexuality. The incumbent of a parish who decides to 'come out' about his sexuality is likely to experience a lack of understanding and even hostility from parishioners because he is the Vicar. The bishop may also be less than sympathetic or supportive to a priest who has chosen to place him in a position which will require a decision to be made in advance of a universal deliberation.

The prevalence of homosexuality in the Church of England

cannot be gauged with any degree of accuracy, and certainly not from the evidence of a sample group of 40 male homosexual clergy who as Fletcher admits were all attending a support group. This evidence does however suggest that as a population group, homosexuals are more likely to suffer stress and strain, and the Church should be mindful of its pastoral responsibilities both as a caring employer, and as a body whose primary function is to proclaim and witness to the all-embracing love of Christ. While those who are married or celibate have enjoyed a recognised status in the Church, homosexuals are left to fend for themselves.

The prevalence and current psychological profile of homosexuals in other denominations is also difficult to assess as there is a paucity of research undertaken with the requisite method and scale to be either reliable or persuasive. Given the degree of anecdotal evidence I would however be surprised if a similar pattern to that found in the Anglican Church did not emerge. In recent years several denominations have attempted to find answers to the questions posed by homosexuality amongst the Church body as a whole. At the time of writing the Church of England is to begin again the work started by the Osborne Committee and the American Presbyterian Church has undertaken a number of initiatives in this area. It would seem to me that at least some of the distinctive tensions felt by homosexual clergy could be reduced once the churches had successfully engaged with these issues at a more general level.

The Ordination of Women may well lead the Church to consider its position with regard to Lesbian priests and how this may or may not differ from that of its present stance with regard to homosexual clergy.

Chapter Three

INTRODUCTION

The person and the environment are part of one inclusive entity. This means that neither individuals nor their settings can be adequately defined without reference to the other, and that the activities of one necessarily influence the other.

The parochial environment is made more complex by its being both static in the sense that it is geographically and historically defined (the parish), and fluid in that its membership (priest and people) is constantly changing and is subject to social, economic, political, and cultural forces which may influence individual behaviour within the parochial setting.

The characteristics of the priest, the form and rules of the setting, and the social and cultural norms all influence the incumbent's 'map' of the setting and what occurs in it. In the setting, the priest behaves (e.g. perceives, interacts, performs), thinks (recollects, calculates, develops impressions), and feels (pleasure, arousal, peacefulness, anxiety), and is healthy or unhealthy. Transactions within the settings have outcomes: the incumbent may be better off (happier, healthier, more skilled), or worse off (overly stressed, ill, angry, frustrated). Some of these outcomes are immediate, others have delayed reactions. Not only is the priest affected by the parish, but often the parish is affected by the priest, as well.

The following Case Studies and Parish Profiles bring both priest and parish together in a way that presents the reader with the opportunity to observe this dynamic interplay of social, societal and individual factors in real-life settings.

CASE STUDIES AND PARISH PROFILES

Permission to include the following case studies has been given to the author by the individuals concerned. Real names have been replaced by fictitious ones and certain alterations have been made to prevent identification.

The first case study is of an interview arising out of the author's data gathering for the update on primary role function in 1985. The interview, which was not tape-recorded, was written up on the same day, and is based upon both recall and impressions, supported by known and verifiable facts concerning the priest and the parish in which he served. The author accepts that a declared interest in psychology and in particular stress-related illness might well have occasioned some degree of 'negative affectivity'.

(1)

Bill is the vicar of St.Anne's, a parish of some 8000 souls in the outer suburbs of an urban sprawl in the West Midlands. He was appointed as incumbent two years ago by his bishop who believed that he could rise to a challenge. Bill is challenged because the parish church had become more and more isolated from the mainstream of community life. The forty or so communicants at the 9.30am 'Family Service' on Sundays (Rite B) are mostly elderly and female.

The red brick building has an adjoining hall which is used for parish gatherings (wedding receptions, scout activities, and Bingo on Wednesday afternoons). Above the hall is a small committee room where the PCC hold their meetings. The vicarage, next to the church, is larger than the surrounding 'semi's' built just prior to and immediately after the second world war; shielded behind a screen of elder and privet, the parson's house is largely hidden from view.

The parish has a fairly even mixture of private and local authority housing, a county primary school, a combined health and day care centre, and a small shopping parade. Where the parish gives way to open farmland there are a few older houses, the middle class occupants of which form the backbone of the Parochial Church Council.

Bill's first six months as vicar were exciting and novel.

People came to church out of curiosity to meet the new man, and to hear what he had to say. Invitations to tea, supper, community gatherings and the like came flooding in.

At first, the PCC meetings under Bill's chairmanship went down very well. When he talked about the Alternative Services, Renewal, Mission, Planned Giving, and Stewardship there was a respectful silence. He was impressed with the efficiency of the Churchwardens (a former headmaster and a Lt.Commander RN Retd.) who, with the PCC secretary and the treasurer, had kept things going during the long interregnum. In his second year Bill began to make a few small changes. To his surprise, he discovered a reluctance to change of any kind. The honeymoon was certainly over!

The crisis point occurred at a PCC meeting some eighteen months after his induction. Bill managed to maintain a calm responsive attitude towards the flood of criticism and complaint which came at him from every side, but he also felt his stomach tightening as the heated debate moved away from the relatively mild changes he had made to the ordering of worship, and centred upon his inaudibility in church, his inability to deal with the outbreak of mindless vandalism in the area, and upon more personal issues concerning his wife, his children, and the untidy state of the vicarage garden.

'What have they got to do with my ministry ?', and, 'How can Christians, of all people, be so uncharitable and petty ?', were questions which he threw at me with some considerable display of emotion at our first meeting.

I had called on Bill, a parson colleague, to ask for his help in compiling a pilot questionnaire for the forthcoming diocesan clergy conference at which as pastoral advisor, I hoped to explore the level of support, loyalty, appreciation, and reward, clergy received in their ministry. As we discussed this, and parish life in general, Bill had became increasingly animated, and it soon became evident that he needed to talk to someone. For the next three hours I listened as Bill poured out a catalogue of experiences and frustrations, some current, some going back to his childhood.

Now in his mid-forty's, Bill was born in 1939. In 1943 his father was reported missing, presumed dead. A presentation scholarship together with a grant from an Army charity, made it possible for Bill to receive a public school education.

Leaving at the age of sixteen he began his working life as a
bank clerk (a nice, safe job, his mother said). Bill lived with
his widowed mother and supported her during the prolonged
illness which preceded her death in 1964.

The local church, was supportive at a time when he needed
sympathy and understanding; and he was drawn more and
more into the worship and social life of his home parish. Bill
was invited to join a lay leadership training course where he
met his future wife, Jennifer, then aged nineteen and in her
first year at university. They had much in common. Jennifer,
also an only child, had recently suffered the bereavement of
her clergyman father.

The decision to offer himself for ministry came after a
Christian Fellowship week at Lee Abbey, which Bill, Jennifer
and their fifteen-month old daughter attended in 1967.

For Bill and Jennifer the 'born again' experience which they
shared was a turning point in their lives, a time for total
commitment to Christ and to each other. I asked Bill to
describe what he felt. 'Euphoria, excitement, apprehension,
and a total sense of inadequacy', he replied.

Jennifer's return from the school run with Sarah, now aged
seventeen, her fourteen year old sister, and ten year old
brother, brought a temporary halt to our talk. I accepted
Jennifer's invitation to stay for tea on Bill's insistence. 'We can
natter afterwards in the study', he added.

The study was minute and over-furnished with a pine desk,
a swivel chair, two metal filing cabinets, an ancient gestetner
duplicator on its stand, and a couple of rexine covered
armchairs. Alcoves on either side of the fireplace had been
fitted with shelves on which were stacked perhaps a hundred
books. I glanced at their titles as Bill busied himself lighting
the gas fire. It was the library of an evangelical progressive
with more than a passing interest in charismatic renewal.
Whatever interests Bill had outside his ministry there was no
indication of them in his reading or in the other visible
contents of his study. The solitary picture, hanging over the
fireplace was a framed photograph of a group of men in front
of a Gothic ivy-clad building. Turning from the fire, Bill
responded to my interest in his college days. As a married
ordinand, his first term had had been anticipated with a
mixture of anticipation and blind panic. What he encountered

when he arrived was a warmth and friendliness from fellow students and staff. Getting to know one another was written into the agenda in those early days.

The frank exchange of biographies, the lengthy discussions about the meaning of life, the sharing, the excitement of being 'alive in God', and knowing Christ as one's personal saviour, created the feeling of being chosen and of belonging.

The initial euphoria was replaced in Bill's third term by a period of internal conflict, marked by a shift in emphasis from the intellectual and ideological to the personal and the emotional. Bill found that he, rather than his knowledge of theology, doctrine, church history and ethics, was the object of examination. A pattern of criticism, self-criticism and confession dominated with increasing intensity. Criticism covered every aspect of thought and behaviour. The slightest show of unorthodoxy or non-conformity was nipped in the bud. Indications of a lack of total commitment and involvement were seen as a mark of personal unworthiness. Standard criticisms repeatedly driven home included individualism, placing personal interests before duty, and allowing one's attachment to family or friends to interfere with one's service to others. Bill was required to accept these criticisms gratefully when they were offered. He was expected both to anticipate and to expand on the criticism of others by self-criticism. The criticism and self-criticism process was extended into virtually every aspect of community life, always with a high moralistic tone. Under attack were the forces of Satan, characterised by pride, conceit, greed, competitiveness, dishonesty and sexuality. Confession compulsion swept the college as ordinands vied with each other in their frankness. Students were encouraged to 'witness' in public and to express relief and thanksgiving at the washing away of their sins in the Blood of Christ.

When Bill, troubled by recurrent bouts of gastric 'flu', insomnia, tiredness and loss of appetite, sought help from his pastoral tutor, he was urged to spend more time in prayer and less on worrying about his health.

Jennifer entered the study with more tea, and was invited to join us. Looking over to Bill and receiving a reinforcing nod, she sat down in the armchair he had vacated in favour of the swivel behind the desk.

'My ears are burning. What have you been saying about

me?', she asked 'Bill has been reminiscing about theological college,' I replied. 'Did Bill tell you about the time I was told to leave the chapel because Sarah and Rachel were making too much noise in Communion? I was furious! But not half as angry as I was when the principal wouldn't allow Bill to stay with me when Sarah had to go into hospital to have her tonsils out'. 'Bill told me about the time you two first met', I answered. (Bill had in fact said very little about his wife and children so far). 'That was in my first year at Uni', Jennifer replied. 'Did you complete your degree?, I asked. Jennifer paused before replying, and looked past me into the distance. 'I was quite keen on teaching, but then Sarah came along, and what with one thing and another.....Perhaps when Paul leaves school'. Her voice trailed away. 'Anyway, I don't think they would be very keen on the vicar's wife going out to work. They think I do little enough in the parish as it is..... I feel absolutely dense these days... and I would have to get my PGCE first.'

'Jennifer's a lot brighter than me. I leave the thinking to her', Bill cut in, as he rose from his chair and edged towards the door. I took this as my cue to leave, and thanked my hosts for their time and hospitality.

Bill walked with me to the car. 'I am so grateful to you for sharing with me'. I left with the hope that Bill and I would have a chance to chat again during the clergy conference. Bill doubted whether he would be able to make it. His back had been troubling him lately, and the tablets which the doctor had prescribed made him feel tired and a bit depressed. He added, 'It's a long drive, and I'm not very good with lots of people around me these days'.

Not all of Bill's stress symptoms, if we accept them as such, may be categorised within the framework of any one stress model. For example the onset of ill-health first manifested itself at a time when Bill was under considerable pressure at Theological College to conform to and identify with a particularly rigid role image of priesthood and ministry, one which would inevitably conflict with the demands of married life and parenthood because of its emphasis upon and demand for total commitment to the exclusion of family needs and personal interests. The harsh and seemingly unjustified criticism and complaint Bill received from the PCC would have compounded any feelings of inadequacy and loss of self-confidence which might have originated from a repressed and fatherless childhood and the demands of caring for a sick mother.

Bill's apparent feelings of guilt about the disruption of Jennifer's career prospects after graduation might well have stemmed from an awareness of how much she had given up in terms of personal ambition and self-realisation in order that he might pursue his vocation.

The total commitment demanded of her husband by the Church at a time of family crisis (when Sarah was in hospital), might well have been for Jennifer the first intimation that the once-shared experience of vocation and dedication was in reality an unremitting sacrifice of personal needs and personal aspirations. Much is expected of a clergyman's wife in the Church of England, and the parson's wife is bound by the same constraints and strictures as her husband.

For married clergy, the home/work interface (see above) is all too frequently a point of conflict giving rise to intense feelings of guilt, frustration and anger. Although the only evidence for this in Bill's case was an insistent clamour for attention from their father on returning home from school, and a studied indifference to my presence, clergy children often do suffer intense feelings of jealousy at having to share their daddy with strangers.

(2)

In the second case study, deep-seated emotional problems acted as a spur to effort and achievement, 'Flight' from an unacceptable self had provided the energy and impetus to engage in a very heavy work-load which brought with it both reward and retribution.

The fear and uncertainty which comes from being ill can produce symptoms of their own. An example of this was presented to me when I visited a colleague who had suffered a coronary thrombosis and was confined to bed. This was the longest period of inactivity Geoffrey had experienced for many years, and the enforced idleness caused more symptoms than the coronary itself. Geoffrey was a very anxious person with a number of unresolved personal problems, most of them having to do with his inability to relate to the opposite sex. He had learned quite early in life to avoid the effects of this inner conflict by immersing himself in academic study, and later his parish and diocesan work. This, up to the present, had been an effective strategy in that it had kept him preoccupied, and had prevented him from dwelling upon his unresolved sexuality.

Geoffrey's capacity for work had brought its own reward with a prebendal stall, membership of the Bishop's council and many important committees in the diocese. He was able to reassure himself that there was little wrong with him in the light of all this personal achievement. To his fellow men he appeared to be a highly active, striving and tense person who they were apt to describe as a 'ball of fire'. The coronary put an end to all this, and lying immobilised in bed Geoffrey's mind turned inwards. He began to have symptoms of acute anxiety in the form of cardiac neurosis on top of the actual cardiac infarct which was without symptoms itself at the time. He developed palpitations, pain over the heart, faintness and shortness of breath.

Treatment consisted of reassurance that he was not about to die, and an explanation of the nature of his symptoms. Then the emotional problems underlying the anxiety were explored and Geoffrey was able to see for himself after a while how his whole life had been one of avoidance and flight from his deep-rooted sexual fears. When these were brought into the open he became a much calmer person, no longer running away from himself, and he was able to take life more as it came.

(3)

Promotion, coupled with little or no participation in decision-making, and conflict with a senior colleague, formerly a close friend, may be identified as likely causes of George's depression and ill-health.

George, a fifty-two year old vicar was conscientious and hard working, but very prone to worry. For many years he had been in a parish that stretched him to the limit. This was acceptable to him, and his relationships with his archdeacon and area bishop were satisfactory. Like most clergymen he received only minimal direction from the diocese, but his bishop and staff at Church House were available whenever the need arose. He experienced a high level of job satisfaction and from this a sense of well-being.

Because of his former teaching experience (and B.Ed.) George was invited to become a full-time member of the diocesan education team in conjunction with an appointment as team vicar in an inner city united benefice. In his new post George found his life constrained and hemmed in by the dictates of others to whom he was accountable (using his highly developed capacity for judgment and decision-making had been a major element in his former work satisfaction).

It was the loss in middle-age of his discretionary responsibility that George felt most keenly, experiencing it as a real deprivation. His relationship with the bishop deteriorated rapidly and he began to feel strained and to sleep badly, often waking during the early morning hours. He later became seriously depressed.

George sought the advice of his GP who, rather than refer him for psychiatric help, intervened with George's consent, directly with the archdeacon, a mutual friend. George, in due course, received an invitation from the bishop to consider the incumbency of a large urban parish where his undoubted skills could be exercised to the full with complete autonomy. In his new role, George's depression lifted rapidly and his health problems largely resolved.

(4)

A rural parish is vastly different to its urban counterpart. Traditional ways and traditional forms of worship perpetuate the age old link between the fruits of the earth, people, and place, and the country church and its place in the community is deeply rooted in a religion which has to do with the agricultural seasons and a propitiatory God. 'He does not belong to these parts', is an accusation which is made of an incomer to this day, in dismissing an unacceptable intrusion into an historically established order and pattern of life. The Church, in its theological training programme, is only now beginning to make provision for the study of rural ministry and its association with the worship of a God who is more distinctly of the Old Testament than of the New (in the past those who entered the Church were often the sons of the landed gentry; whereas today ordinands are more likely to come from middle-class city and suburban families).

Peter found himself in an alien environment, confronted and challenged by a role set which was impossible to fulfil. He neither recognised the expectations of those around him, nor had the experience to cope with the transitions he was asked to make.

Acting on advice from his doctor, Peter, the vicar of a large suburban parish, sought a light-duty post following major abdominal surgery. The bishop was sympathetic to Peter's needs and appointed him priest-in-charge of a rural parish which was eventually to become part of a united benefice upon the retirement of a neighbouring incumbent.

Peter tried very hard to adapt to country ways. The previous vicar had been a very keen gardener and the contributor of a weekly article on natural history to the local newspaper.

Peter was not a gardening man and the vicarage garden and four acre orchard which had been the pride and joy of his predecessor soon became a wilderness.

The quiet reserve of his parishioners puzzled him. They never seemed to get enthused about anything or take the slightest interest in the establishment of week-day services (the old vicar in all his thirty years kept worship to a minimum with Morning Prayer at 11am on Sundays, and Holy Communion twice a month at 8am).

Peter's arrival in the parish coincided with a number of resignations, and in his first year he had to find a new PCC treasurer as well as a new secretary; and he was warned that the Vicar's Warden would not be standing for re-election at the next vestry meeting. Fortunately, a housing redevelopment scheme centred on redundant farm buildings in the village, brought new blood into the community, young professionals who were prepared to 'get involved'. 'Newcomers should not go running things as though the place belonged to them', said the Parish Council chairman, voicing public opinion.

The new hymns, the 'family service', the accent on young people – bringing them into the life of the church – which went down so well in Peter's old parish fell flat, and Peter found himself more and more isolated from his flock.

Peter was not the only one to feel the growing rift between the village and the parsonage. Peter's wife found herself left out of things. She was treated almost as though she were an alien from another planet; the more she tried to get to know her neighbours, the more her intentions were misunderstood. 'Poking her nose in', was how she once heard her endeavours described.

A letter of complaint was sent by the People's warden to the bishop, accusing Peter of failing to maintain the traditions of the parish in matters of ritual and worship. The bishop agreed to meet the vicar and parishioners in the parish church at an open meeting.

The accusations levelled at Peter seemed in the light of day to be of little substance, but nevertheless they added up to a situation which was damaging both to the parish and to the priest.

The bishop spoke warmly of Peter's strengths, and of how, in his previous parish, he had brought a once dead church to life, and had revitalised the community by his dedication and enthusiasm. To touch upon their sympathy and Christian charity, the bishop confided that Peter had worn himself out physically by overwork and unstinting service to others; Sally had given her all in support of her husband's ministry, and her home was an open door to anyone who needed a cup of tea and a friendly ear. 'Peter', he continued, 'may not be a countryman, he may not fully understand your ways, but he is a true man of God, and is entitled to your love and acceptance as a servant of Christ'.

An uneasy silence followed the bishop's observations.

After a lengthy pause, the bishop added, 'In the light of what has been said and what has been left unsaid, I shall do everything I can to help Peter to find a parish which will merit his very special talents'. The meeting closed with prayers and a blessing.

Peter, shortly afterwards, had to undergo more surgery, and was given the benefit of early retirement.

PARISH PROFILES

The Church's current crisis of identity has had a measurable effect upon the attitudes, perceptions, job satisfaction, level of perceived stress, and coping style of Anglican clergy which can be directly attributed to environmental factors which are present in differing parochial settings. Evidence for this has come from

*Davey, J.(1989) Priest and Parish: A psycho-geographical perspective of Anglican Parochial Ministry today. Ph.D. thesis, Univ. of London.

a field survey (Davey:1989)* which sought to redress the imbalance of previous research by concentrating upon the following questions which had not been posed in previous studies.

1. What particular attitudes and perceptions do today's clergy have in relation to their ministry, and why have they come to adopt them ?
2. Are these related to current Church strategies, especially with regard to the amalgamation of benefices, and changes in ministerial emphasis ?
3. Where have these changes been felt most ?
4. How have clergy responded to changes in their occupational environment (i.e. levels of perceived stress and coping styles) ?
5. What action might the Church take in response to the perceived attitude and expectations of its clergy ?

Answers to the above questions which are directly related to the function and office of priesthood today, have a value over and above other surveys by providing an assessment of the effect which current ministerial strategies have had upon clergy working within differing occupational environments.

Specific factors which were perceived to inhibit or enhance personal (ministerial) objectives were found to be significantly related to the type of benefice in which incumbents exercised their ministry. Each category of ministry was examined (rural, urban, single, multiple) with the aim of quantifying and qualifying the relationship between the incumbent's perception of role, level of support, reward, appreciation, and job satisfaction, the value placed on ministerial effort, and type of parish.

Reward factors in ministry are linked to the vocational nature of the priestly role. The choice of suitable work dimensions was, therefore, confined to the measurement of perceived reward in terms of difficulty, challenge, variety, interest, opportunities for advancement, workload, sense of achievement, fairness, involvement in decision-making, and ministerial effectiveness.

Job satisfaction is traditionally assessed in relation to the feelings that an individual has about the job itself (e.g. the nature of the work, the rewards it offers – including pay and promotion, the degree of autonomy or supervision it provides, and the level of support and appreciation received from employers and colleagues); a view which owes much to the human relations school of management. Locke (1969)*, however, emphasises the concept of value fulfilment. Satisfaction, in Locke's view, occurs when the job fulfils what one values. The 'Action Tendency' approach advocated by Locke, such as 'If you were starting over again in your career, would you choose your present employment?' his more likely to provide a reliable response than direct ratings of feelings. The Job Satisfaction measure therefore employed this approach in measuring 'vocational satisfaction' as a factor in relation to particular parochial settings (see below).

JOB SATISFACTION
THE QUESTIONNAIRE
High/low

1. NO YES   When you wake up in the morning do you often feel reluctant to commence work?
2. YES NO   Do you ever feel reluctant to cease work at the end of the day?
3. NO YES   Do you often feel like breaking off from what you are doing for a rest or refreshment?
4. YES NO   Are you sometimes reluctant to leave the parish to go on holiday?
5. YES NO   When you are on holiday do you often wish that you were back in the parish?
6. YES NO   Do you ever wish that your day-off was over so that you could get on with your work?
7. YES NO   If you were starting over again in your career would you choose the parochial ministry?
8. YES NO   Would you commend the parochial ministry to an ordinand/prospective ordinand?
9. NO YES   Do you ever wish that your Bishop would invite you to consider another 'Living'?
10. NO YES   Do you ever feel tempted to leave your present parish?
11. YES NO   Do you think that you will be reluctant to retire when the time comes?
12. NO YES   Would you consider early retirement if you were given the opportunity?
13. NO YES   If alternative work in the Church were offered you, would you accept it?
14. NO YES   Have you ever regretted your choice of career?

*Locke, E.A. (1969) What is Job Satisfaction? in Organisational Behaviour and Human Performance, 4. 309-336

The accompanying table shows a significant relationship between perceived attitude in relation to ministry, and type of parish.

A ranking of the means by type of parish not only provided an indication of the extent to which certain benefices conformed to a pattern of responses, it also enabled a direct comparison to be made between differing ministerial settings and their characteristic features. Single parish rural benefices within the Church of England are rare today and incumbents of this group tend to be older than their professional colleagues; many, in fact were appointed prior to the 1976 legislation which required clergy to retire at the age of 70.

Multi-parish rural benefices have arisen out of the dearth of vocations, and the adoption of the 'Sheffield' formula which ensures that clergy are appointed to areas of greatest need. The amalgamation of parishes to form united benefices under one incumbent has created a heavier work-load which is reflected in the significantly lower reward ratings for incumbents in this sub-group.

Incumbents of single parish urban benefices are in the main younger than their professional colleagues, and their drive and enthusiasm is consistent with their overall perception of ministry as challenging, interesting, appreciated and supported. The Church has promoted the city parish as the battle ground and front-line of mission and the greater degree of support given by the Bishop to incumbents in the multi-parish urban category of benefice reflects this fact.

The ranking of means for reward, support, and appreciation, is uniformly consistent within benefice categories; with single-parish urban benefice incumbents perceiving a significantly greater reward, support and appreciation factor in their ministry than their multi-parish rural benefice colleagues.

Findings for Support/Appreciation (involvement in the social life of the parish) are an exception which may be explained by the fact that incumbents of Multi-parish rural benefices have a social standing and role in more than one community which would tend to heighten their perception of social involvement.

The overall ranking of the General Health factors by benefice category is fairly close to that recorded for reward, support, and appreciation.

RANKING OF MEANS BY TYPE OF PARISH

REWARD	S.R	M.R.	S.U.	M.U.
Difficulty	2	1	4	3
Challenge	3	2	4	1
Variety	3	1	4	2
Interest	3	2	4	1
Workload	2	1	4	3
Sense of achievement (job)	2	1	4	3
Fairness	1	3	2	4
Involved in decision-making	1	2	3	4
Opportunities for advancement	4	1	3	2
Physical surroundings	3	4	2	1
Ministerial effect	4	1	2	3

SUPPORT				
Support by Bishop	2	1	3	4
Support by Archdeacon	3	1	4	2
Support by Rural Dean	2	1	4	3
Relationship with fellow clergy	4	1	3	2
Relationship with church officers	2	1	3	4
Lay visiting support	3	1	4	2
Lay ministry	4	1	3	2
Support from PCC	1	2	4	3
Clergy support effectiveness	4	1	2	3

APPRECIATION				
Appreciation from parishioners	3	1	4	2
Appreciation from the hierarchy	2	1	4	3

SUPPORT/APPRECIATION				
Involved in the social life of the parish	1	4	3	2

GENERAL HEALTH				
Physical Exercise	4	2	1	3
Bodyweight	1	3	2	4
Psychiatric/counselling help	3	2	1	4
Receiving medication	4	1	3	2
Blood pressure	4	1	3	2
Tense/nervous/anxious	1	3	4	2
Level of smoking	4	3	2	1
Alcohol consumption	3	2	4	1
Health status	1	3	4	2
Time-off	3	2	1	4

JOB SATISFACTION	2	3	1	4

(1 = lowest overall mean, 4 = highest overall mean)

Categories: S.R. Single parish rural benefice   (8 benefices)
              M.R. Multi-parish rural benefice   (21 benefices)
              S.U. Single parish urban benefice   (32 benefices
              M.U. Multi-parish urban benefice   (13 benefices)

The single-parish urban priest has the highest grade for health status, but is younger.

There are few surprises in the general findings (above); for example, one would expect a correlation between the support of the Bishop and reward factors such as challenge, and involvement in decision-making. However the significance of the rural dean in aspects of challenge and sense of achievement is interesting, indicating perhaps, that the support role of the 'next in line' is of importance. Opportunities for advancement are significantly related to support from the Archdeacon (who fulfils a particular role in the Bishop's council on recommendations for preferment). Interpersonal relationships, in terms of support and appreciation would therefore appear to play an important part in aspects of reward and general health in Anglican parochial ministry.

The environmental matrix (see overleaf) qualitatively relates the comments made by incumbents concerning aspects of their ministry to particular parochial settings, firstly by category of benefice, and secondly by type of parish.

Half of the comments made by incumbents were critical of the organisational aspects of the Church of England, the majority of which were from incumbents of multi-parish and rural benefices.

About a third of the total referred to ministerial and parochial problems, this time coming mostly from incumbents of single-parish urban benefices. Personal problems which had an occupational bearing accounted for about one fifth of the issues raised, two-thirds of which were from incumbents of multi-parish rural benefices.

Multi-parish incumbents expressed more frequently the view that multi-parish benefices inhibited their pastoral ministry (this group also referred to competing priorities which led to, as one incumbent put it, 'an army of rushed and jaded clergy'. Personal problems, especially related to ill-health, were also referred to most frequently by incumbents of this category of benefices.

Synodical Government was considered by many incumbents of single-parish urban benefices to be largely ineffective and far removed from the 'grass-roots' of parochial ministry. Too many changes too quickly, the level of bureaucracy, and an inadequate stipend for the level of responsibility, was

ENVIRONMENTAL MATRIX

The first table (1) is a topic list of the personal comments made by clergy when asked to identify particular problems and anxieties relating to their ministry. The second table (2) is a grid which relates the topic frequency to types of parish.

(1) Topic List

Organisational
Hierarchy remote and impersonal.
Lack of support from above.
Ineffective leadership.
Lack of consultation on major issues.
Ineffective communication system.
Increasing bureaucracy.
Increase in the number of non-parochial appointments.
Too many changes too quickly.
Synodical Government remote from 'grass-roots'.
Training for parochial ministry inadequate.
Unfair system of preferment and promotion.
Inadequate stipend for level of responsibility.

Ministerial and Parochial
Too much time spent on administration.
Multi-parish benefices inhibit pastoral ministry by duplication of effort and repetition.
pastoral reorganisation counter-productive.
Fund-raising for essential repair work to ancient fabric is a drain on local resources.
Competing priorities
Diminishing lay appreciation and support.
Conflicting expectations - lay/hierarchical.
Inflexibility of parochial system.

Personal
Ill-health.
Tied accomodation.
Dual Career conflict.
Work/Family conflict.
Clerical Isolation
Moonlighting*

(2) Frequency Grid

	TYPE OF PARISH**(% RESPONSE)				
	S.R.	M.R.	S.U.	M.U.	Total
ORGANISATIONAL	50	58	31	25	50%
MINISTERIAL/PAROCHIAL	20	25	28	25	30%
PERSONAL	30	30	6	19	20%

* Moonlighting (taking on additional paid work such as teaching) has become more widespread in the Church as stipends fail to keep up with the rise in the cost of living.
** Refer to page 62 for category and population sample for each type of benefice

commented on by more than one incumbent in this category.

A qualitative comparison of the problems associated with ministry in relation to type of benefice highlighted some specific factors, such as higher work-load, associated with multi-parish incumbency. A number of individual incumbents referred to problems which they had encountered in their own ministry. Such comparisons are, however, of less value than the consensus of a group of clergy exercising their ministry in similar occupational settings.

These findings are consistent with the Gallop (1986) survey, which also pointed to the predominance of organisational factors in clerical discontent.

Summary of parish difference

The questionnaire findings (including the ranking of means) together with the correlation coefficients and comments made by incumbents provide an overview of parochial ministry today as it is enacted within differing parochial settings. The high/low comparisons are in relation to other types of benefice.

Single-parish rural benefices

The comparatively low ranking given to 'involvement in decision-making by this group may be compared with an expressed desire for greater lay participation in ministry at the parish level. Feelings of isolation are expressed in the low ranking given to involvement in the social life of the parish, whereas relationships with fellow-clergy is ranked highly.

For many clergy in this group the regular Clergy Chapter meetings provide support and fellowship which may be lacking elsewhere. This is reflected in the relatively high ranking for clergy support effectiveness in contrast to the ranking for the support which the incumbent receives from the PCC.

The comparatively high ranking for ministerial effectiveness suggests a high self-image, which the low reported ranking for health status and high ranking for 'tense, nervous, anxious,' does not support. Four out of the eight incumbents in this group were receiving or had received psychiatric or other help.

An apparent inconsistency is the high ranking given to

'opportunities for advancement'. why this may be so may be related to the fact that the benefices represented were prestigious (six incumbents had been involved in at least four career moves).

Poor leadership from above – with change for change's sake, increasing bureaucracy and an under-valuing of parochial ministry – were specifically mentioned, together with criticisms of an ordination training programme which fails to provide either theological colleges or relevant experience in the North of England.

The low ranking given to fairness of stipend is supported by the reference to 'moonlighting' to augment income. The cost of living in country areas was reported to be higher than elsewhere (Russell & Nott:1986),* yet in spite of this many dioceses exercise a stipend differential in favour of town and city parishes.

The personal comments of clergy in this category of benefice are illuminating; for example, the reported low health status is attributed by two incumbents in the open-ended section of the questionnaire, to lack of support and friendship in the parish, loss of ministerial direction, and not being in control of one's time and work programme. This lead in one case to the taking of early retirement at age 59, and in the other, to resignation from a previous benefice due to a nervous breakdown.

The Gallup Survey (1986) found that overall clergy have a perception of their own state of health as being better than the national average, with 46% describing their health as very good, 37% as good, and only 20% as fair or poor. This applied equally to Urban Priority Areas and Non UPA's. Likewise, Fletcher (1990)† found that the psychological health of clergy was significantly better than general population norms. The number of single parish rural benefices is small in comparison to other types of benefice and one needs to exercise caution in the interpretation of the findings which might reflect a sampling artifact; however, previous studies have not differentiated between categories of benefice.

*Russell A. and Nott P. (1986), *A Rural Strategy for the Church of England.*
†Fletcher, B. (1990) Clergy under Stress. London: Mowbray

Multi-parish rural benefices

Support and appreciation are reported by clergy of this group, to be lacking from both the hierarchy and the parish, in spite of this they record a low ranking for their ministerial effectiveness. Their involvement in the social life of the parish is high. The intensive parochial activity may be costly for some in terms of general health, a view which is supported by the ranking for blood pressure.

Those who accept 'livings' in the country are aware that this may preclude them from advancement in the Church and this may account for the low ranking for 'opportunities for advancement'. One incumbent commented that getting on in the Church depended on who you know and not what you know. The low ranking given to support and appreciation is substantiated by criticisms of the hierarchy for their remoteness, indifference, and lack of interest. In the absence of effective and 'caring' leadership and support from above, clergy expressed a lack of confidence in their own ability to set goals and objectives. One incumbent admitted to periods of doubt and depression, and difficulty in reconciling the roles of priest and parent. Too many decisions were being made, said one incumbent, by those who lacked parochial experience, and parochial ministry was being devalued. This view was supported by others who criticised the 'draconian' changes enforced by church bureaucracy such as the amalgamation of parishes which was driving worshippers away. One incumbent commented on the unfairness of the stipend and how tied accommodation made it difficult to buy one's own home for retirement.

The incumbent who stated that he was 'totally fulfilled' in his present ministry went on to express his concern that a move would be disastrous for his wife who had her own career as a teacher and 'loves it here'.

Another incumbent expressed his frustration at being in a rural parish when he would have preferred to be in an urban one, ' being unable to force a rustic wife and family into an urban situation'. The high ranking given to physical surroundings and ministerial effectiveness is reflected in one incumbent's statement that ' being a parish priest in the Church of England is the most privileged position in the world, and we get paid for it! The strength of the Church is still in the parishes'.

The above comments illustrate the mixed attitudes of incumbents in rural benefices, the 'forgotten priests' identified by Russell (1986)* who have 'little voice and less power to effect changes in either the Church structure or their own careers'.

Single-parish urban benefices

The mean comparative age of incumbents in this benefice group is 48 years. Many of the 33 questionnaire variables relating to aspects of reward, support, and appreciation, received top ranking from this group, including sense of achievement, and health status. Physical surroundings, which are given a comparatively low rating, are not compensated for by 'time off' from the parish. The ratings for 'advancement', and 'relationships with fellow clergy' suggest an optimistic view of future career prospects.

On self-percept evidence alone, this type of parish would appear to offer a yardstick for other ministries. The personal comments of incumbents of single parish urban benefices who hold positions of strength and influence in the Church, however, contain a number of observations which are highly critical of the 'system', including the view that 'probably the Church of England has finished its useful life', and 'pastoral reorganisation should be much more drastic'.

An awareness of the problems which can arise from lack of consultation is voiced in the comment that decisions should not be left to those who have no real experience of the real-life parish. Parochial ministry is seen as the backbone of the Church, not Bishops and their administrative apparatus, least of all the Synod and the Church Commissioners. A number of incumbents commented on conflicting expectations and competing priorities in a role which is ill-defined in terms of status, territory, and responsibility.

The incumbent who wrote, 'I just get on with the job. I did not come into ministry for promotion, money, popularity, and an easy time; the Bishop, Rural Dean, and Archdeacon are of little consequence or significance to me', shows an indepen-

*Russell, A. The Country Parson. London: SPCK

dent outlook in comparison to that of a colleague who commented that 'clergy, whilst nice people, are not up to the job they are doing'.

Multi-parish urban benefices

The high ranking given to 'involvement in decision-making and 'relationships with church officers' is contrasted by the low ranking given to 'appreciation' from parishioners, in spite of a comparatively high work input. 'Opportunities for advancement' and 'relationships with fellow clergy' are ranked on the low side in contrast to that of single parish benefice incumbents. A low ranking is given to 'challenge', 'interest', and 'physical surroundings'. There is a significant cluster of low rankings for 'level of smoking', 'alcohol consumption', and 'bodyweight', with a correspondingly low ranking for physical exercise.

Time-off is also given a high ranking. Complaints voiced by incumbents of this group include, 'too much time is taken up with fund-raising, maintenance of fabric, and administration.'

Defining priorities of work, motivating people, and having 'too many people to care for', is encapsulated in the statement by one incumbent that 'we are in danger of sinking beneath the waves'.

There are topics common to all incumbents regardless of differing types of parish; each benefice however, represents a unique pattern of interaction between priest and people. The following parish profiles give an insight into the day to day problems which clergy face in their ministry. They are reported as they were conducted, using the outline interview schedule below:

1. Demographic
2. Perceived role of the Church
3. Primary role of the incumbent
4. Principle perceived problems

The comments made by the participant incumbents imply various coping tactics employed in response to the presence of factors which were perceived to be stressful and sometimes counterproductive to an effective and fulfilling ministry. The coping classification (direct action/palliative) which was suggested by Lazarus has been adopted in the presentation of the parish profiles.

Single Parish Rural Benefice (1)

1.   Medium size market town predominantly middle-class
Population: 4500
Incumbent   : Married, aged 41
Average Sunday attendance (all services): 350
Support from:-
Hierarchy: very good
PCC: very good
Parishioners: very good

2.   Role of the Church in the parish:
To encourage people to come to church

3.   Incumbent's primary role:
'My role is to lead the people in worship, to celebrate the Mass daily, to visit my parishioners, and to create some kind of unity between them. They are not really united in anything except conservation issues and the threat of over-development.'

4.   Principle problems:
'Isolation. I am on my own.'
N.B. When asked to elaborate, the above incumbent replied that the relative wealth of his parishioners created a barrier between himself and them. He could not afford to return their hospitality and therefore no longer accepted invitations. Visiting without a good reason, e.g. baptisms, a wedding or bereavement, was often construed as an appeal for charity. 'It's the Vicar, can you get my purse/wallet', was an instinctive response, he felt, to his appearance at the door.

Single Parish Rural Benefice (2)

1. Large village in stockbroker belt
Population: 2000
Incumbent: Married, aged 34
Average Sunday Attendance (all services) 65
Support from:
Hierarchy: poor
PCC: good
Parishioners: reasonably good

2. Role of the Church in the parish:
To stimulate spiritual awareness.

3. Incumbent's primary role:
Pastor, counsellor, and representative of Christ.

4. Principle problems:
'Mobility, a constantly changing population. We are failing to attract young people to church.'

OBSERVATIONS:

(1) The relatively high church attendance figure in the first parish reflects the 'fit' between the role of the Church as the 41 year old incumbent sees it, and the way in which he has translated this role into activity. The incumbent is confident that his ministry is successful. The objective, 'encouraging people to come to church' is being accomplished. Societal expectations are maintained within accepted parameters. This incumbent is engaged in both 'direct action' coping in terms of pastoral activity, and 'palliation' in avoiding social encounters across an economic divide.

(2) The young incumbent of the second parish interprets the Church's role as that of awakening spiritual awareness. His primary role is in keeping with that perception. As 'representative of Christ', and as pastor and counsellor, the main thrust of his ministry would appear to be that of 'presence'. The attendance figures would suggest the local church is engaged in a 'holding' activity with little real support or enthusiasm from parishioners; a view which is strengthened by the comment that people are 'moving away', and young people are not coming to church. A palliative coping style is suggested by the role which the incumbent has adopted – 'like a rock which is submerged at every flooding tide.'

Multi-Parish Rural Benefice (1)

1. Large coastal village – 2 churches
Population: 4000
Incumbent: Married, aged 54
Average Sunday Attendance (all services) 60
Support from:
Hierarchy: Reasonably good
PCC: Reasonably good
Parishioners: Reasonably good

2. Role of the Church in the parish
'The Church has an important part to play in community life.
Visiting and pastoral care is still expected in the villages. The
strong 'folk religion' element must be educated (N.B. the
incumbent is here referring to those parishioners whose attendance at church is seasonal); Churches are full at Christmas
and Harvest Thanksgiving. But what happens to the people on
other Sunday's in the year ?'

3. Incumbent's primary role
'I am essentially a building maintenance man. Almost all of
my working energy is put into keeping the church dry warm,
and rot-proof. I am still clearing up the churchyard after the
storm of '87.'

4. Principle problems
'The church is starved of resources. The stipend is far too low,
and the expenses of office fall largely on me.'

Multi-Parish Rural Benefice (2)

1. Stockbroker belt village – 2 churches
Population: 1700
Incumbent: Married, aged 63
Average Sunday Attendance (all services) 65-70
Support from:
Hierarchy: good
PCC: very good
Parishioners: very good

2. Role of the Church in the parish
'The Church should be rooted in the countryside. Its priests should be versed in country ways and customs. Its leaders prepared to speak out against falling moral standards and acts of vandalism'.

3. Incumbent's primary role
'I was trained as a pastor and that is how I see myself.'

4. Principle problems
'fewer young people means that the church is far too dependent on older people do everything. The Church in my villages is like a club, pretty exclusive.'

OBSERVATIONS:

(1) The multi-parish rural benefice incumbent has many problems to contend with in exercising a ministry which is fragmented, repetitive, and time-consuming. The first incumbent in this category was overwhelmed by the task of maintaining the fabric of two historic buildings. Visiting, pastoral care and religious education were seen as the Church's primary role and yet the incumbent had neither the time nor the energy to accomplish these objectives in the benefice. This failure to fulfil the interpreted role is reflected in poor church attendance and the complaint that he is starved of resources. This incumbent has failed to cope with the pastoral problems associated with his 'cure' and has directed his activities to the fulfilment of a substitute role, which is that of 'maintenance man'.

(2) The incumbent of the second multi-parish rural benefice has been in his present 'living' for the past twenty years and has gathered around him a loyal band of regulars who, like himself, are traditional in outlook. His churches are rather like an exclusive club. The perception of a Church which is rooted and grounded in the concept of a pastoral God is reflected in its patristic, wise and venerable local representative. The church attendance figure is high (4% of the population) in comparison to the national average (2.5%).

Single Parish Urban Benefice (1)

1. Large coastal town
Population: 4500
Incumbent: Married, aged 40
Average Sunday Attendance (all services) 120
Support from:
Hierarchy: Good
PCC: Good
Parishioners: poor

2. Role of the Church in the parish:
To witness to the presence of Christ

3. Incumbent's primary role:
'To administer the Sacraments and to provide facilities which the State refuses to fund, like a play group and an adult learning centre.'

4. Principle problems:
'The widening gap between the have's and have not's. The Church is the only hope for the poor. The Government have got to listen to us and be made aware of their responsibilities.'

Single Parish Urban Benefice (2)

1. Suburban middle-class area of coastal town
Population: 6000
Incumbent: Married, aged 54
Average Sunday Attendance (all services): 160
Support from:
Hierarchy: Good
PCC: Good
Parishioners: Reasonable

2. Role of the Church in the parish:
'leaven in the lump; being there.'

3. Incumbent's primary role:
'Motivator and enabler; inspirer.'

4. Principle problems:
'In my parish there is very little sense of community. There is
no focus. Everyone goes to the centre to shop and to find their
amusement. The place is dead by seven o'clock in the evening.
I am an anonymous figure representing a lifeless corpse. Yes,
people come to church here, but they don't want to get
involved. Church going is largely a habit with most of them.
Visiting ? They would rather be left alone.'

Single Parish Urban Benefice (3)

1. The adjoining parish to the above
Population: 7800
Incumbent: married, aged 52
Average Sunday Attendance (all services) 200 +
Support from:
Hierarchy: very good
PCC: very good
Parishioners: very good

2. Role of the Church in the parish:
'To evangelise'.

3. Incumbent's primary role:
'To support the team and provide resources for the work of
evangelism'.

4. Principle problems:
The hierarchy is totally out of touch with the parishes and fails
to support its ministers at the grass-roots level. What has been
done in this parish is a team effort. If you cannot involve
people and give them something to do they will not stick.
Unless the Church can attract young people it will die on its
feet.'
    N.B. There is a contradiction in the views expressed, and
the perceived support received from the hierarchy.

OBSERVATIONS:

(1) The first incumbent in this category of benefice related his
pastoral activity to the perceived role of the Church by exercis-

ing a sacramental ministry and providing a social service to the community. Attendance at church services was slightly above the national average. The fiery idealism of this forty-year old cleric was matched to an environmental climate which was challenging. The expressed frustration and anger of a zealous priest with a social conscience has been channelled into 'direct-action' coping in providing facilities for the disadvantaged.

(2) The second incumbent in this category is an older man faced with the challenge, not of social deprivation, but of indifference. Church-going was a 'habit' rather than a spiritual experience to most of his congregation. A suburban middle-class parish is almost by definition church-going which is what the Sunday attendance figures reflected. The palliative coping of this incumbent reflects his perception of the Church's role, yet at the same time is contradictory to the role he ascribes to himself as enabler and inspirer.

(3) In the adjoining parish to the above, the incumbent has gathered a team of dedicated Christians around him. His role was that of team leader and enabler. Evangelism was the declared role of the Church. Sharing of responsibility and total involvement created an atmosphere of success. In reality the church attendance figures were no better than the national average. An 'us' and 'them' attitude prevailed which was reflected by the failure of the hierarchy to support the parishes. They were seen to be 'out of touch'. The 'sharing' need of this incumbent reflects a defensive coping style which is dependent on support and comfort-seeking (reinforcing the status quo) in the face of a growing sense of ineffectuality.

Multi-parish Urban Benefice (1)

1. Large county town close to the capital
Population: 8000
Incumbent: Married, aged 52
Average Sunday Attendance (incl. daughter church) 150
Support from:
Hierarchy: poor
PCC: very good
Parishioners: very good

2. Role of the Church in the parish:
'To proclaim the Gospel and to act as a catalyst.'

3. Incumbent's primary role:
'To give a lead, and to get things going.'

4. Principle problems:
'Rootlessness. people come and go in this parish and its difficult to keep track of things. Family problems take up a lot of
my time. That and the funerals account for most of my pastoral
work here. Things get started up, like the Bible study, but
people don't know when to call it a day, and it goes on and
on. The same old faces week by week.'

Multi-parish urban benefice (2)

1. Large coastal town – Urban Priority Area:
Population: 12/13000
Incumbent: Married, aged 49
Average Sunday attendance (all services – incl. daughter
church) 170
Support from:
Hierarchy: very poor
PCC: good
Parishioners: very good

2. Role of the Church in the parish:
'To give hope to the poor and to feed the hungry in the name
of Christ.'

3. Incumbent's primary role:
'Finding resources and funding for the 'centre'.'
N.B. The above parish is engaged in an Urban Priority Project
to provide shelter for destitute and homeless people who grav-
itate to this popular seaside town from all over the country.
The church crypt has been equipped as a dormitory and soup
kitchen.

4. Principle problems:
'A large number of single-parent families live in the parish.
Alcholism and drug abuse is a major problem in the area and

the police cannot provide enough presence to keep the streets safe at night.'

Multi-parish urban benefice (3)

1. Large coastal town – Urban Priority Area
Population: 15000
Incumbent: Unmarried, aged 46
Support from:
Hierarchy: very good
PCC: very good
Parishioners: good

2. Role of the Church in the parish:
'Helping people towards God's Grace; meeting people half-way, loving them.'

3. Incumbent's primary role:
'Offering a sacramental ministry and being dedicated and committed oneself.'

4. Principle problems:
'My health is not that good, and there is a limit to what I can do. We have a scheme going here which takes up a lot of my time, and it provides the churchwardens with something worth-while to get their teeth into. Its hopeless, really. There is not one pane of glass left on the south side of the church.'
   N.B. The church crypt is used as a drop-in centre for the homeless and social misfits. On the day of my visit eight people were in the centre, four of whom were church officials, including the churchwardens, the Vicar, and a Church Army parish worker.

OBSERVATIONS:

The Multi-parish benefice clergy visited faced an overwhelming task of ministering to populations of between eight and fifteen thousand souls. Their pattern of ministry was dictated, to some

---

*Davey, J.(1984). Research Project for the BSc. (hons) Degree. Univ. of London.

extent by the size of the benefice; and low church attendance reflected the scant level of individual pastoral care which can be achieved in parishes of this size (see Davey:1974)*

The first incumbent of this group saw the role of the Church to be that of proclaiming the Word of God. This was interpreted literally by the establishment of a successful Bible Class which provided a point of contact for the Vicar and his congregation. The comment about 'seeing the same old faces' underlines the frustrations of establishing contact with a predominantly mobile and 'rootless' society. The 'direct-action' coping adopted by the incumbent seems to have misfired, and added further to his sense of being in a rut.

Two of the parishes visited were multi-parish urban benefices with populations in excess of 12000 and designated as Urban priority Areas. In the first case the incumbent had interpreted the role of the Church to be that of social provider. The establishment of a soup kitchen and dormitory for the destitute gave both the Church and its incumbent a role in the locality. The Church was seen to be doing something and thereby assumed a credibility which it would not otherwise have had. Church attendance was considered to be relatively good, although it fell far short of the national average. This incumbent is coping by 'direct-action', redefining his role in social directions. His answer to a localised situation reflects that of the Anglican Church in its policy statement encapsulated in 'Faith in the City'.

The second UPA provided a contrast to the former. With a population of 15000, the incumbent was overwhelmed by the sheer magnitude of his ministerial task. The church building, which was kept locked, had become the target of vandals who had smashed virtually every pane of glass in the windows. The sacramental role of the Church was reflected in the incumbent's commitment and self-dedication. The establishment of a drop-in centre for the homeless and social misfits provided a role for the incumbent and church officers which would otherwise have been non-existent. The church attendance figures for this parish were the lowest recorded (0.2%). The ill-health referred to by the incumbent was directly attributable to factors which were present in his occupational environment, which made him feel depressed, tired, and drained of energy. The 'palliative' coping had failed to reduce or eliminate his stress level but short of leaving his present living or changing his personal ideals of priesthood, there was little else he could do.

The above findings, because they are grounded in real-life situations, provided evidence of the link between the attitudes adopted by individual clergy and the parishes in which they exercised their ministry. In general, when the primary role function of ministry as perceived by the incumbent, is out of touch with reality, an external attribution style has been adopted, and personal misgivings were expressed in terms of the problems which were associated with particular parochial environments; for example, rootlessness, no sense of community, lack of resources, and social deprivation. The tension which exists between the manifest and latent functions of ministry is most acutely felt by those priest who are called to exercise a sacramental and teaching ministry; the falling numbers of worshipping members must create a vacuum which is difficult to fill. The role reversal which is required of them under present ministerial strategies fails to satisfy either their vocational calling or their ability to respond to a change in attitude with regard to their perceived priestly function.

Individual response dispositions.

Individual differences were reflected in a number of ways; e.g. in the role conflicts exemplified by the pastoral priest who spent most of his time and energy on maintenance, the priest who valued unity and community identity and yet felt isolated by the social barrier created by the relative wealth of his parishioners, and the inspirer and enabler ministering to people who did not want to be involved and would rather be left alone.

Negative affectivity is the disposition to react to stress with negative emotional states. High NA individuals tend to be chronically distressed and upset and have a negative view of the self. The negative mood states experienced by NA individuals include nervousness, tension, and worry; anger, scorn, revulsion, guilt, and self-dissatisfaction; a sense of rejection, and sometimes sadness, are some other examples of the affective states associated with NA. In contrast, those low on the NA dimension are relatively content and secure and satisfied with themselves. Individuals disposed to anxiety react more strongly to stressful situations; in the absence of stress they tend to be no more anxious than those low on NA.

In an earlier study (Davey:1984) a significant positive relationship between neuroticism and multi-parish incumbency was found. Incumbents of multi-parish urban benefices visited by me in the course of the field study also expressed varying degrees of anger, frustration, rejection, tension and anxiety. It would seem from the evidence of these studies that multi-parish urban incumbency is counter-productive to both the spirit of the pastoral system and to the ability of individual priests to relate to more than one ecclesiastical community (the parish) with any degree of ministerial effectiveness.

The incumbent of the first single parish urban benefice might be described as a 'hardy' personality type with a transformation coping style 'aimed at not only survival but also the enrichment of life through development' (Kobassa et al:1981)*.

Hardy' persons have considerable curiosity and tend to find their experiences interesting and meaningful; they believe they can be influential through what they say and do, and expect change to be the norm, regarding it as an important stimulus to development.

However, people low on 'hardiness', tend to find themselves and their environments boring, meaningless, and threatening, feeling powerless in the face of overwhelming forces or pressures for change; when stressful events occur, these have a debilitating effect on their health and well-being.

*Kobassa, S.C., Maddi, S.R., & Courington, S. (1981) Personality & Constitution as mediators in the stress-illness relationship. *Journal of Health and Soc. Behaviour*, 22, 368-378

Chapter Four

Clergy Support

INTRODUCTION:

In virtually all the current literature relating to occupational stress, there is an emphasis upon the shortcomings of organisations with regard to their management style and management systems, these shortcomings often resulted in a perceived lack of support from above, and a correspondingly high level of perceived stress among employees.

Although many dioceses provide counselling and support where the effects of stress have become overwhelming, stress management initiatives still remain largely within the province of the individual. Seeking help from others may not be easy for those who are reluctant to admit that they are under stress, or who may feel that an admission of stress may compromise their future career prospects. An integral part of any stress management programme is the identification of particular stressors associated with the work environment and the home/work interface. The table below (Stressful Characteristics of Work: Cox et al 1993)*, although not clergy specific, illustrates the relationship between those work characteristics which are associated with management styles and management systems, and the resultant conditions which may give rise to perceived stress. As a first step in the establishment of a viable stress intervention and management programme, the Church as an employer will need to acquaint itself with those stressors within the occupational environment which are pertinent to ministry, and to

*Cox, T. et.al (1993) Occupational Health: Control and Monitoring of Psychosocial and Organisational Hazards, *Journal of Royal Society of Health* Roy. Soc. Health Aug. 1993

identify particular situations and particular individuals who may be susceptible to the environmental/situational conditions which may give rise to perceived stress.

STRESSFUL CHARACTERISTICS OF WORK

WORK CHARACTERISTICS	CONDITIONS
ORGANISATIONAL STRUCTURAL, FUNCTION & CULTURAL	Poor task environment Poor problem solving environment Poor development environment Poor communication
PARTICIPATION/CONTROL	Low participation in decision making Lack of control over work
CAREER DEVELOPMENT	Career uncertainty Career stagnation Poor status or status incongruity Poor pay Job insecurity and redundancy Low social value at work
ROLE IN ORGANISATION	Role ambiguity Role conflict High responsibility for people
JOB CONTENT	Ill defined work High uncertainty in work Lack of variety or short work cycles Fragmented or meaningless work Underutilisation of skill Physical constraint Continuous exposure to client/customer groups
WORKLOAD/WORK PACE Quantitative & Qualitative	Lack of control over pacing Work overload or underload High level of pacing or time pressure
WORK SCHEDULE	Shift working Inflexible work schedule Unpredictable work hours Long or unsocial work hours
INTERPERSONAL RELATIONSHIPS AT WORK	Social or physical isolation at work Lack of social support at work Interpersonal conflict Poor relationships with superiors
HOME/WORK INTERFACE	Conflicting demands of work and home Low social or practical support at home Dual career problems

Stress Management:

There are times when the only person to suffer the adverse effects of stress will be an individual facing a personal crisis who needs immediate help and support. But stress seldom effects just one person; far more frequently, the stress experienced by an individual has a ripple effect which is felt by a much wider group which includes immediate family and friends, clergy colleagues, parishioners, and society at large.

If one accepts that stress is endemic in ministry, its effect will be experienced throughout the Church. Interventions aimed solely at the individual may be likened to the first aid applied to combatants. Effective human resource management demands more than this from those who are responsible for the health and well-being of the troops in the front line.

WHO KNOWS ... ABOUT THE PROBLEM ?

The victims of stress will be aware of their own levels of anger, frustration, worry and distress. They may feel powerless and have no insight into the extent of the problem, but they do know that something is wrong. Furthermore their behaviour may be dysfunctional and counterproductive to effective ministry.

Senior clerics may also be aware of the effects of workload and change both on themselves and their clergy; and the Bishop, the Archdeacon and Rural Dean will be conscious of the human costs involved in organisational response to social change and budgetary constraints (e.g. pastoral reorganisation and withdrawal from traditional areas of ministry in education, industrial mission, and so forth).

Support agencies, counsellors and close colleagues, may have personal experience of the consequences of stress on others, but as this lies within the domain of client confidentiality, its extent and level within the diocese will largely be hidden from view.

WHO CAN ... DO SOMETHING ABOUT THE PROBLEM ?

There are three distinct approaches to answering the above question: namely,

1. Who can approve and make available the resources required – including time and appropriate people ?
2. Who can influence the management style of the Church, so that it is seen to be more supportive of its clergy?
3. Who can provide the practical skills and knowledge to make a real impact on the problem ?

An appropriate stress management model for the Church will be dependent for its success on a high level of organisational commitment, the support of colleagues, the involvement of professional agencies, and effective monitoring and evaluation.

IMPLEMENTATION

Implementation has two broad thrusts. First, there must be the acceptance on the part of Church leaders that stress levels are unacceptably high and counter-productive to effective ministry, leading to a commitment to do something about stress reduction. Secondly, there needs to be the establishment of a support structure for clergy (and family members) who are experiencing stress. Members of the support group will need to have the skills required to work in a client-centred way, which means:-

- traditional counselling and listening skills,
- an ability to work in a way which empowers others and does not foster dependency,
- a commitment to helping people to explore their own issues and develop their own strategies for change,
- and, knowing when it is appropriate to refer.

The role of senior clerics is to identify such people, help them develop the necessary skills, and provide ongoing support.

The Health and Safety at Work Act of 1974 provided the impetus for proactive thinking about health issues and risk management in the U.K. The systematic problem-solving approach adopted in the wake of the former legislation on health and safety at work has been made explicit in the new directives for the Control of Substances Hazardous to Health 1988 (COSHH) and the subsequent amendment (1990). The continuing theme throughout COSHH is the need to adopt a formalised and systematic approach, and the requirements of COSHH are set out in the following six steps.

1. identification of hazards,
2. assessment of associated risk,
3. implementation of appropriate control strategies,
4. monitoring of effectiveness of above strategies,
5. reassessment of risk, and
6. review of information and training needs of employees exposed to hazards.

The above control cycle may be applied to the management of stress with equal effectiveness, adopting a model proposed by Cox et al (1990).

1. The acceptance that employees are experiencing problems of stress at work,
2. the analysis of the stressful situation, with the identification of the psychological, organisational, and other hazards involved, and the nature of the harm that they might cause,
3. the assessment of the risk to health associated with those hazards,
4. the design of reasonable and practical control strategies
5. the planned implementation of those strategies, and
6. the monitoring and evaluation of the effects of those strategies feeding back into a reappraisal of the whole process.

Management Models

The following stress management models, 'A' and 'B', contain the core ingredients of a stress management programme.

Model 'A' is reactive in that it addresses the needs of clergy who are in all probability suffering from the adverse effects of stress.

An effective sickness monitoring system will identify clergy who are suffering from stress-related disorders and also pinpoint probable causes. Sickness monitoring can also lead to the identification of specific work stressors and particular parochial environments which may be the cause of perceived stress among the clergy.

To achieve this aim, it is recommended that:-

(1) Initial notification be the responsibility of Rural Deans by way of a quarterly pro-forma identifying deanery clergy who may be at risk and who show obvious signs of stress.

(2) Identification of cause.

(3) Initiating stress intervention/support programme.

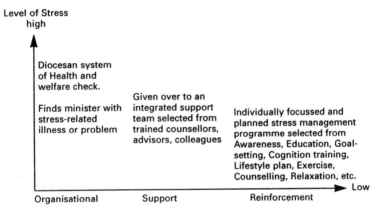

STRESS MANAGEMENT – MODEL 'A'

Level of Stress
high

Diocesan system
of Health and
welfare check.

Finds minister with
stress-related
illness or problem

Given over to an
integrated support
team selected from
trained counsellors,
advisors, colleagues

Individually focussed and
planned stress management
programme selected from
Awareness, Education, Goal-
setting, Cognition training,
Lifestyle plan, Exercise,
Counselling, Relaxation, etc.

Low

Organisational   Support   Reinforcement

STRESS MANAGEMENT – MODEL 'B'

High Levels of Stress – Impaired Performance

Recognition
Policy
Resources
Budget
Implementation Plan
Education
Awareness
Training
Prevention Strategy
Annual Review

Support from
colleagues, Rural
Dean, Diocese,
Counselling Special
Agencies

Feedback, cont.
support, Recreation,
Job Change, Life-
style change

Sickness levels
Early retirement,
Early Death

Low

Organisational   Support   Reinforcement   Monitoring

(4) Monitoring progress.

(5) Follow-up related to (2)

(6) Appropriate action taken in consultation with the Archdeacon or Area Bishop in the case of long-term stress-related illness or absence from the parish.

Redeployment, rehabilitation, exit from, or continuation of the stress management programme, will be determined by a periodic review of individual progress.

The proactive approach to stress management outlined in the Stress Management Model B (above), is dependent on the recognition that stress can not only impair the health and well-being of individual clergy, but also lead to a decline in pastoral care. The first stage in stress reduction is diocesan recognition, leading to the adoption of a policy which includes resourcing, appropriate training, and a prevention strategy. The second stage relates to the quality of support received by individual clergy from colleagues, senior clergy , and ancillary agencies. Additional support should be provided in the form of counselling by trained personnel. The reinforcement aspect of stress management is centred on personal and professional development through appropriate training, and personal well-being.

Supportive Care

Many of the problems currently facing the clergy today may be directly attributable to a lack of support, sympathy, understanding, and appreciation in one form or another. The failure to provide an effective support network in ministry which includes problem and anxiety sharing between the incumbent, the hierarchy, colleagues, and parishioners, can only lead to an increase in both perceived stress in ministry and its somatic consequences.

Supportive care focuses on present realities and present situations. Helping clergy to cope with and accept here and now problems, is an important landmark in the process of building up a repertoire of successful coping strategies to be carried forward and used in the future. To achieve the right balance between authority and care will be both demanding and rewarding; to be successful, senior clergy must themselves be equipped with the necessary skills and techniques.

1. The senior cleric must be able to gratify dependency needs which include comforting, sustaining, guiding, protecting, instructing, and setting parameters of acceptable behaviour (both can communicate caring)

2. The acceptance of another's concerns and anxieties by:
a) Listening, b) Sharing, c) Caring,
To sense that a respected authority person knows and cares about you as an individual brings powerful feelings of having one's life undergirded.

3. The supportive relationship will engender confidence and trust, allowing others to gain enough objectivity to view problems with greater insight and to explore alternatives which are feasible.

4. The senior cleric must have the authority and be in a position to advise when it is necessary and beneficial to change a life situation when that life situation becomes too debilitating, frustrating and inhibitory.

5. When clergy are stunned or paralysed by feelings of defeat, fear of failure, damaged self-esteem, or tragic loss it is often helpful to prescribe some form of activity which will keep them in touch with people and functioning. This reduces the tendency to depression and withdrawal from relationships.

   Projecting what might be, what could be, and what is hoped for, can be extremely beneficial as an exercise in 'writing one's own prescription'. Like all supportive measures this should be used selectively in cases where clergy require the support and encouragement of authority to carry out an activity which is necessary or promising for personal growth and well-being.

6. Suggesting courses of further study and specialist training and providing the necessary resources in terms of funding and time-off, can be extremely beneficial in circumstances where a priest has reached an inspirational or creative low. Practical help and support at this time gives meaning and purpose to the supportive relationship.

   Most dioceses already provide a support structure which includes the availability of trained counsellors who are able to give confidential advice, and guidance to clergy, members of their immediate family, retired priests, clergy widows, and dependents. The area bishop, archdeacon, or designated carer, is also able to offer help and advice on a wide range of problems, including finance and debt, problems and difficulties in the parish, domestic worries and interpersonal relationships, retirement, and bereavement.

Group and Team Ministry

'Teamwork, with shared vision, shared objectives and, where appropriate, shared protocols, is essential if the range of skills, and the resources to deploy them are to be channelled to the maximum benefit of people in the most cost-effective ways', is the view of the task group established by the Parliamentary Under-Secretary of State for Health, when considering the future of nursing services in the context of primary health care.

The Church, as it moves towards the fulfilment of Our Lord's command that 'We should be one', both in the long-term objective of Church Unity, and the short-term experimentation with shared resources and shared ministries at the local level, should also seek ways to maximise on team effectiveness by a greater understanding of the ways in which groups function and the psychological constraints which may impair overall group performance.

Under the Pastoral Measure (1983), provision is made for the establishment of Team and Group Councils (S.I.1981 No 959):-

A Team Ministry comprises a Rector and one or more Team Vicars, who share the 'cure of souls', and may have other lay or ordained ministers who share in 'the pastoral care'. There will be a single benefice comprising one or more parishes. The Rector may have a freehold or a term of years, while all other members of the Team must be licensed or given permission by the Bishop. In the case of Vicars their license must be for a term of years.

A Group Ministry comprises a number of incumbents or priests-in-charge of independent benefices. They must meet as a chapter, the chairman of which may either be elected or appointed by the Bishop.

In either case there may be a Council-Team or Group relating to the area as a whole exercising such powers as may be thought to be appropriate in each case.

A case for Team and Group Ministry (in which some 10% or

more of the clergy are involved indirectly in one form or another) has been made on the grounds that:-

1. Social changes have encouraged teamwork where previously the individual has been dominant. Changes in attitudes to authority where the style of the single authoritarian leader has been radically questioned in the name of greater participation, have led many to seek the authority that comes from corporate decision-making rather than relying on the single authority figure. At the same time in an increasingly complex society, it has been difficult if not impossible for any one person to keep abreast of developments and new research in their field and often teams of specialists have replaced the single lone professional.

2. Declining numbers of clergy have meant that each ordained minister is bound to be faced with greater areas of responsibility. If pastoral care is to be provided adequately, and if the mission of the Church is to be furthered then every parish priest will have to find ways of sharing functions of ministry with others, especially since the ideal of each community having its own parish priest has largely broken down, especially but not exclusively in rural areas.

    For this reason it has become necessary to establish ways whereby a number of people can cooperate in providing ministry for a group of parishes. If such arrangements include a number of clergy then this may allow the different gifts of individuals to be utilised to the full and to compliment one another, while they will also give parishioners the opportunity to encounter a variety of styles of preaching and ministry.

3. The theological background to collaborative ministry comprises two main areas: (a) Ideas about community expressed in the Old and New Testaments; (b) Ways in which these themes developed in practice, particularly in the history of the early Church. Teamwork in ministry is part of a wider concept. The theme of the solidarity of a person with other people, with the world of nature, and with God, runs with consistent strength through the Bible and is a reflection of the nature of God himself.

4. In Biblical history, the community mattered more than the individual. Whilst personal responsibility is a real element,

modern ideas about individuality and privatisation were foreign to Jewish thought. A person's significance was realised only in and through the life of the community.
5. Just as the concept of community is dominant in the religion of the Old and New Testaments, so the idea of ministry as a corporate rather than an individual vocation is an underlying assumption.

The main criticisms levelled at Group and Team ministries, as set out in the General Synod Report (GS 660) are that:-

a). It is often said that team and group ministries sometimes fail to take account of the geographical and sociological realities of a locality.
b). It is suggested that teams and groups can encourage in certain clergy a new form of clericalism which results from the clergy's close involvement in the internal organisation of the team and with each other which further separates the clergy from the laity and from the wider society.
c). It may lead to the exclusion of the laity from decision-making.
d). Team and Group ministries infringe upon the professional independence of the clergy and inhibits the individual relationship between the priest and the parish.

The research findings of West and Slater (1995)* indicate that personality factors can hamper group decision-making, with dominant individuals exercising excessive influence over decisions or solutions even when their solutions were incorrect. The popular expectation is that group decisions will be superior to those made by individuals working alone. However, the research evidence is consistent in suggesting that the quality of group decision making generally equals but does not exceed the quality of decision making of the average member. The quality of decision making of the most able members is generally not matched. Those with potentially excellent input into the decision-making process may often be inhibited from putting their ideas forward or their ideas may be ignored because they have lower status or are less dominant.

*West, M.A. & Slater, J.A. (1995) The Occupational Psychologist. No. 24. April 1995

The intervention strategy focus in team building should be on defining clear objectives for the team, improving role understanding and skill use, identifying specific performance problems, and devising detailed action plans to deal with presenting problems.

In their study of Team Effectiveness, Guzzo and Shea (1992)* concluded that:-

Individuals should feel that they are important to the fate of the group.

Individual tasks should be meaningful and intrinsically rewarding.

Individual contributions should be identifiable and subject to evaluation and comparison.

Teams should have intrinsically interesting tasks to perform.

There should be clear group goals, with in-built performance feedback.

Stress in Teams: The success of a team depends upon the quality of the interaction between its members and the extent to which individuals can work together and support each other.

The team leader needs to be aware of the danger signs which will give an advance warning of stress build-up:

Tasks not achieved,
sickness, absence, unpunctuality,
covering up mistakes,
cold or hostile atmosphere,
little trust or reliability,
deadlines not met,
backbiting, gossip,
some members not pulling their weight,
poor communication,
work below an acceptable standard,
lack of cooperation between members,
power struggles.
put-downs, and
high staff turnover.

*Guzzo, R.A., & Shea, G.P. (1992) Group Performance and Inter-group relations in Organisations. Journal of Personality & Social Psychology, 53, 497-509.

The problem may be related to the maladaptive response of one member of the team to pressure, or it may be associated with a lack of clarity or understanding about what the team is aiming to achieve.

Stress is rather like a virus; if an individual feels under pressure and responds to that pressure by going sick, becoming overbearing, argumentative, irritable, or irrational, this will effect the rest of the team. The outcome is poor individual performance and increasing pressure upon others to shoulder the load.

Dependency relationships:

How team members relate to each other is an important aspect of stress management. 'Who depends on whom?', and, 'how does the performance of one individual help or hinder another?', are questions which may help to identify and clarify the factors which may inhibit the accomplishment of the team goal.

A constituent part of team building is to ensure that the right people are brought together, and that each member has the appropriate skills and experience for the job in hand.

A team can be viewed as a group of people who just happen to work together, either because of what they do or by the nature of the organisational structure. Alternatively a team can be seen as a source of creative energy with a high potential for problem solving and task accomplishment. Successful organisations know how to make teams work, how to utilise differences, how to harness energy and commitment, how to minimise the effects of harmful stress brought about by unrealistic demands and work overload, and how to generate the dynamic of healthy challenge and pressure to bring about optimum performance.

To succeed and at the same time be 'stress fit', attention needs to be given to the 'How's' of team structuring :

How it is put together (and disbanded)
How people are inducted into and leave it
How it organises its work as a whole
How an individual's work connects with and is dependent on others

How it communicates, reviews, and evaluates performance
How people feel about their team membership

A healthily stressed team -

Creates and makes most of the challenge
Works together by
Using conflicting views and achieving synergy
Balances the pressures within the team, and finds ways to build up support
Monitors its achievements
Learns from its mistakes
Maximises on individual skills
Develops skills to enhance future performance
Makes full use of available resources, with each member
Contributing to his or her highest potential.

Too little variety in the team task will, for some members, lead to boredom and frustration, which may result in unconstructive activity. For others, too much activity can generate a stress level which is counter-productive to team effectiveness. Assessing the skills, experience and job demands of each team member against the following check-list can be helpful in diminishing the likelihood of stress build-up.
What skills and experiences are needed for the team to succeed?

What skills and experience do we have?
What do we have too much of?
What do we have too little of?
Who has too much to do?
Who has too little to do?
Whose skills and experience are being under-utilised?
Who is being overstretched?
How can we rearrange the way we operate?

Understanding the work demands of each member of the team, and finding ways to meet pastoral targets through team working, will help to communicate respect and support and thereby build up team confidence and individual self-esteem.

The Management of Change

As the Church moves towards a period of rapid and radical restructuring it is essential that the skills required to effect good management practice and to facilitate change are widely known and widely employed.

The management of change, supportive counselling within a management framework, and an effective monitoring and review procedure form an integral part of an overall stress management programme.

Advocates of change may try to bring about alternative patterns of ministry to meet the same needs, or to meet them better, and to counter areas of dysfunction by sanction or the adoption of schemes of accountability (appraisal) which may either seek to maximise on human resource power or on individual skills and aptitudes.

Functionalism does, however contain a warning for reformers – in that existing institutions may be serving hidden functions (e.g. manifest and latent functions) and it is important to understand these hidden functions before changing things too much. An example of this is the shift in emphasis from ministry as a vocation and an expression of a life-time dedication to the work of the Lord, to that of a service staffed by professionals who are tasked to perform specified objectives and attain certain goals. A job for life, embodied in the 'parson's freehold' might well reflect, on the part of some individuals, a life-time of service in a parish, whereas a fixed-term contract and membership of a ministerial team, might not hold the same appeal.

Functionalists emphasise that functions cannot be equated with individual purposes or motivations; the functions of ministry are objective consequences, which may be quite different from the motivation. In terms of the corporate function of Church, the spiritual care and pastoral oversight of the family of God, and winning souls for Christ, individual satisfactions and the attainment of personal goals might well become subservient to the group task and organisational objectives.

Plant (1987)* proposed six key activities for the successful implementation of change:

---

* Plant, R. (1987) Managing Change and Making it Stick, London: Fontana/Collins

The management of change requires a corporate response based upon the recognition of individual needs and how these needs may be met.

What about the incumbent who cannot see any personal advantage in the changes proposed by Church or Diocese ?

The rethink process in the wake of change requires a radical shift in both the way we think about the ministry (cognition) and the way we are asked to exercise that ministry in the future (behaviour).

The demands of change, the options and the outcomes – both positive and negative, are tabulated below:

The demands of change upon the individual

- TO LET GO OF OLD HABITS.
- TO RESTRUCTURE ONE'S PERCEPTIONS OF THE WORLD.
- TO RESTRUCTURE ONE'S SELF-IMAGE.
- TO SEARCH OUT NEW SKILLS.

Options

- DENY IT.
- FANTASISE ABOUT IT, LOOK TO THE FUTURE
  OR LAMENT THE PASSING OF A GOLDEN AGE.
- HIDE AWAY IN INTELLECTUAL THEORIES.
- FIGHT IT, BE OBSESSIONALLY STUBBORN,
  AUTHORITARIAN, AND DOGMATIC.
- RITUALISE ONE'S LIFE PATTERNS AND LET ONE'S
  ROUTINES THINK FOR YOU.

Negative Outcomes

- REMAINING ENSNARED WITHIN THOSE BEHAV-
  IOURS WHICH RESIST CHANGE AND SO CAUSE
  SELF LIMITATION AND PERSONAL STAGNATION.
- INDULGING IN FEELINGS:- VULNERABLE OR
  DEPENDENT, PERSECUTED, WEAK, POWERLESS;
- PROTECTING ONE'S WEAKNESSES RATHER THAN
  WORKING THROUGH THEM TO NEW STRENGTHS.

Flow with change

- GIVE ONESELF PERMISSION TO STAY WITH
  UNCERTAINTY.
- ACCEPT ONE'S FEELINGS AS ENERGIES AND
  POTENTIALS.
- WITNESS THE PLAY OF FORCES WITHIN YOU,
  RATHER
  THAN SELF-INDULGE AND STICK IN ONE PLACE.
- REFLECT UPON PREVIOUS CHANGES AND HOW YOU
  GENERATED POSITIVE OUTCOMES FOR YOURSELF.

Positive Outcomes

- BECOMING AWARE OF YOUR PERSONAL
  DEFENCES AND DEVELOPING THE TRUST TO RISK
  GIVING THEM UP.
- ALLOWING FRESH INSIGHTS TO DEVELOP FROM
  WITHIN YOU;
- SHARING YOUR 'PROCESS' WITH OTHERS.

- WORKING ON THOSE AREAS OF YOURSELF WHICH DISSATISFY YOU.
- WORKING THROUGH AND THROWING OUT BEHAVIORAL PROPS WHICH YOU HAVE RETAINED FROM THE PAST.

To minimise anxiety and stress among the clergy, the change strategy should include the following:

Core Needs (Organisational and Individual)

- CONTINUITY COMBINED WITH EVOLUTION.
- GROUP IDENTITY AND TEAM BUILDING
- CORPORATE GOAL SETTING
- RECOGNITION OF PERSONAL WORTH AND IDENTITY
- RECOGNITION OF STRENGTHS AND WEAKNESSES
- TRAINING AND INDUCTION
- PERFORMANCE MONITORING
- SKILLS ACKNOWLEDGMENT
- APPROPRIATE REWARD STRUCTURE
- DECISION-MAKING PROCEDURES
- PROCESSES FOR DEALING WITH FRICTION
- STRESS MANAGEMENT PROGRAMME

Guidelines for effective change management

The most frequent criticism levelled at the Church hierarchy with regard to the implementation of change is the lack of prior consultation:

All who are likely to be involved in the change process should:-

- be brought into the change process at the earliest opportunity.
- be consulted about their thoughts and feelings,
- participate in the planning, and in the discussions relating to implementation, particularly with regard to projected time scales.
- have the objectives clearly explained to them.
- have the opportunity to make their own contribution.
- have the above duly acknowledged

MINISTERIAL ACCOUNTABILITY

Ministerial accountability may be viewed either as an organisational expediency and an exercise in 'man' management, or as an endeavour to provide support to clergy and their dependents. The distinction between the two is not at all clear. To present both arguments, the Bishop, for his part cannot assume that he has done everything possible to bring about an effective pastoral oversight upon the appointment and licensing of an incumbent to a parish, neither can an incumbent assume that his or her pastoral and interpersonal skills are such that there is no room for improvement.

The Diocesan schemes of accountability which have been introduced are, in the main, of a voluntary nature. Where they have been linked to an already existing hierarchical 'oversight' there is a danger that clergy might see the additional organisational input as threatening. 'Top Down' schemes of accountability (or appraisal) are invariably suspected by the clergy of being organisational task performance exercises with the aim of maximising on resources and efficiency at the cost of the welfare of members. This negative attitude might be considered as no more than a reaction to the rapidly changing nature of the ministerial role and the increasing pressure to accede to the implementation of diocesan pastoral reforms, which have all too often brought in their wake increased workloads, changing pastoral boundaries, the wholesale disposal of 'plant', and a paring down of available 'man-power' in key areas of ministry by withdrawing the help of assistant curates.

A 'Bottom up' approach to accountability which involves the incumbent and the parish, rather than the diocese has many advantages. Agenda sharing and corporate decision-making, when it becomes an accepted feature of parish life, has the immediate effect of reducing the level of apathy and indifference on the part of those members of the church council who feel that they are insufficiently involved in the decision-making process. Looking forward and planning positively for the future are placed within the context of a group effort.

'What are we here for?', 'What are we setting out to do?', and 'What are our strengths and weaknesses?', are questions set for consideration; the answers become the launching point for the defining of purpose, the identifying of aims, and the projection of viable strategies.

	Material	Cognitive	Social Emotional	Behavioural
The Church Hierarchy	Training	Advice by experts	Support by experts	Support in office
	Clergy	Counsellors	Counsellors	Suggest change
	Stipend	Consultants	Consultants	Grant early retirement
	Housing			Remove from office
	Pension			
The Parish P.C.C.	Expenses of office	Group problem solving	Problem	Practical help
	People (unpaid)	Pooling experience	Support	Sharing responsibility
	People (paid)	Advice by experts	Loyalty	Providing relief during illness/ holiday

The clergy support model (above) proposes that support in ministry can be divided into two broad categories, Material and Psycho-Social. The extent of the material support which the Church can give to its clergy is limited by the current shortfall between resources and expenditure. The psycho-social support, which can be divided into cognitive, emotional and behavioural inputs is less constrained, and can be extended to the clergy at both the diocesan and local level.

Material support lies in the provision of resources for ministry such as training and skills enhancement, and equipment such as computers which can be used for word-processing, record-keeping, project planning, and so forth. Psycho-Social support includes the provision of help and advice from experts, counselling from a trained and trusted colleague, and the provision of a 'locum' to cover duties over a period of in-service training, sabbatical leave, annual holidays and sickness. The parish is seen as the place where the greatest support is likely to be given to ministers. The parish is where clergy will receive their work-satisfaction and sense of vocational fulfilment (important reward factors). The church council is identified as the primary support group outside the immediate family. Agenda sharing, target setting, joint responsibility in decision-making, accompanied by periodic review, evaluation, and merited praise-giving, are seen as positive factors in ministerial support. The importance of feedback, and periodic review, together with reaction to and criticism of each phase undertaken in pursuit of the parish objective, cannot be over-emphasised. Whilst it is relatively easy to create a group whose membership consists of individuals with a common purpose, it is not so easy to control conflicting personalities and negative interaction between members. An incumbent is, by right of office, leader of the church council. In certain circumstances the chairperson can delegate the 'chair' to another. When this happens however, the immediate effect might be to create confusion among members of the council who will be torn between the natural identification of the 'parson' with pastoral leadership as shepherd of the flock, and loyalty to the task leader. An example of this is the way in which sub-groups and sub-committees which are formed as task orientated bodies frequently become splinter groups with a fierce loyalty to the task performance. Church Choirs are notorious in this respect; when conflict arises between the Director of Music and the Incumbent, resignations and bitter acrimony are the order of the day and loyalties become strained and confused.

ACCOUNTABILITY AT THE LOCAL LEVEL

Accountability and appraisal at the local level will be of far greater significance in the future as the Church moves towards the creation of a structure which will depend less and less on historic resources and more and more on local resources for its continuing work of ministry.

Much is expected of the parish priest. Not surprisingly, those expectations cannot always be fulfilled, for generally speaking, ministerial strengths lie in more otherworldly directions.

The most telling of the 'parson's shortcomings lies in the area of leadership skills, and experience has taught that those who do exhibit such skills are unlikely to remain as parish priests for long.

The Church hierarchy is in a position to improve the leadership and social skills abilities of its clergy by providing appropriate training. Far too frequently, however, either because of the absence of suitably qualified practitioners to pass on their skills to others, or the pressure of work on clergy which prevents them from setting aside the time to acquire these skills, there is an inevitable shortfall between the skills expectation of parishioners, and the level of competence of their parish priest in these essential areas of pastoral care.

The following sections on interpersonal skills are included, therefore, to give an overview of human resource management as it relates to pastoral ministry.

LEADERSHIP SKILLS:

The Church Council: Key Questions

- What is the Leadership style?
- What is the Decision-Making process?
- How involved are members in discussion, problem-solving, decision-making?
- How formal/informal are procedures?
- What procedures exist to reinforce and support team working?
- How are people judged? On what criteria?
- How often does the church council meet?
- How are decisions and actions communicated?

The above questions should be addressed at the outset of an incumbency in the form of a group exercise involving the parish priest and members of the church council, and concluding with an 'action plan'.

Goals

- What are the parish objectives?
- How clear are they?
- Are the objectives in priority order?
- What are the 'action' implications?
- What is the level of commitment?

Interpersonal Relationships

- What are relationships like?
- How open are members?
- Do members 'play games', or are they direct with each other?
- Are there any personal animosities or feuds?
- What is the 'atmosphere' like?

Roles:

- Where do people fit in?
- How do roles fit with others (Overlaps, clashes)?,
- What is expected of members, by me and of me?
- How competent do I feel as leader?

ROLE FUNCTIONS IN A GROUP*

What individuals do to serve group needs may be termed functional roles. Statements and behaviours which tend to make the group inefficient or weak may be called non-functional behaviours.

Some of the role functions required in selecting and carrying out a group task are outlined below:-

A. TASK ROLES

1. INITIATING ACTIVITY: proposing solutions, suggesting new ideas, new definitions of the problems, new attack on the problem, or new organisations of material.
2. SEEKING INFORMATION: asking for clarification of suggestions, requesting additional information or facts.
3. SEEKING OPINION: looking for expression of feeling about something from the members, seeking clarification of values, suggestions of ideas.
4. GIVING INFORMATION: offering facts or generalisations, relating one's own experience to the group problem to illustrate points.
5. GIVING OPINION: stating an opinion or belief concern-

---

* Reproduced with permission: National Police Staff College, Bramshill.

ing a suggestion or one of several suggestions, particularly concerning its value rather than its factual basis.

6. ELABORATING: clarifying, giving examples or developing meanings, trying to envision how a proposal might work if adopted.

7. CO-ORDINATING: showing relationships among various ideas or suggestions, trying to pull ideas and suggestions together, trying to draw together activities of various subgroups or members.

8. SUMMARISING: pulling together related ideas or suggestions, restating suggestions after the group has discussed them.

B. GROUP BUILDING AND MAINTENANCE ROLES (functions required in strengthening and maintaining group life and activities).

1. ENCOURAGING: being friendly, warm, responsive to others, praising others and their ideas, agreeing with and accepting the contributions of others.

2. GATEKEEPING: trying to make it possible for another member to make a contribution to the group by saying, 'we haven't heard anything from Jane yet,' or suggesting limited talking time for everyone so that all will have a chance to be heard.

3. STANDARD SETTING: expressing standards for the group to use in choosing its content or procedures or in evaluating its decisions, reminding the group to avoid decisions which conflict with group standards.

4. FOLLOWING: going along with decisions of the group, thoughtfully accepting the ideas of others, serving as audience during group discussion.

5. EXPRESSING GROUP FEELING: summarising what group feeling is sensed to be, describing reactions of the group to ideas or solutions.

C. BOTH GROUP TASK AND MAINTENANCE ROLES

1. EVALUATING: submitting group decisions or accomplishments to comparison with group standards, measuring accomplishments against goals.

2. DIAGNOSING: determining sources of difficulties, appropriate steps to take next, analysing the main blocks to progress.
3. TESTING FOR CONSENSUS: tentatively asking for group opinions in order to find out whether the group is nearing consensus on a decision, sending up trial balloons to test group opinions.
4. MEDIATING: harmonising, conciliating differences in points of view, making compromise solutions.
5. RELIEVING TENSION: draining off negative feelings by jesting or pouring oil on troubled waters, putting a tense situation in wider context.

From time to time, more often perhaps than anyone likes to admit, people behave in non-functional ways that do not help and sometimes actually harm the group and the work it is trying to do. Some of the more common types of such non-functional behaviours are described below:

D   TYPES OF NON-FUNCTIONAL BEHAVIOUR

1. BEING AGGRESSIVE: working for status by criticising or blaming others, showing hostility against the group or some individual, deflating the ego or status of others.
2. BLOCKING: interfering with the progress of the group by going off on a tangent, citing personal experiences unrelated to the problem, arguing too much on a point, rejecting ideas without consideration.
3. SELF-CONFESSING: using the group as a sounding board, expressing personal, non-group-orientated feelings or points of view.
4. COMPETING: vying with others to produce best idea, talk the most, play the most roles, gain favour with the leader.
5. SEEKING SYMPATHY: trying to induce other group members to be sympathetic to one's problems or misfortunes, deploring one's own situation, or disparaging one's ideas to gain support.
6. SPECIAL PLEADING: introducing or supporting suggestions related to one's own pet concerns or philosophies, lobbying.
7. SEEKING RECOGNITION: attempting to call attention to

oneself by loud or excessive talking, extreme ideas, unusual behaviour.

There is a pattern in team formation which has the following characteristics:

FORMING:	There is anxiety, dependence on a leader, testing to find out the nature of the situation and what behaviour is acceptable.	Members find out what the task is, what the rules are, what methods are appropriate.
STORMING:	Conflict between sub-groups, rebellion against leader, opinions are polarised, resistance to control by group; conflicts over intimacy.	Emotional resistance to demands of task.
NORMING:	Development of group cohesion, norms emerge, resistance overcome and conflicts patched up, mutual support and development of group feeling.	Open exchange of views and feelings:cooperation develops.
PER-FORMING:	Interpersonal problems are resolved, interpersonal structure is the tool of the task activity, roles are flexible and functional.	Emergence of solutions to problems, constructive attempts at task completion, energy is now available for effective work; this is the major work period.

GROUP DYNAMICS

Stages:

1. The stage of defensiveness. This is usually at the outset of a group. Trust is low, anxiety is high, and the group dynamic may get locked into one or more of the three restricted forms – educationally alienated, culturally restricted, psychologically defensive. Wintertime: the ground may be frozen, and the weather stormy.
2. The stage of working through defensiveness. The group is now under way, trust is building, anxiety is reducing. A fresh culture is being created. Springtime: new life starts to build through the surface crust.

3. The stage of authentic behaviour. The group is deep into its real destiny. Trust is high, and anxiety is a spur to growth and change. There is openness to self and others, risk-taking, working, caring, sharing. There is flexibility in moving between different strands of learning. Leadership is shared, with a good balance of hierarchy, cooperation and autonomy. Authentic behaviour has many varieties and can include any of the positive forms of the group dynamic – described below. Summertime: there is an abundance of growth, and the sun is high.

4. Closure. As the group draws to a close, the members gather and review the fruit of their learning, and prepare to transfer it to life in the wider world outside. At some point in this process separation anxiety will loom – the distress at parting after such trust and depth of interaction. It can slip the group back into defensiveness unless dealt with awarely - first by accepting that the end is nigh, secondly by dealing with any unfinished business, thirdly by celebrating each other and what has gone on, fourthly by saying a warm, friendly farewell in the group and one-by-one. Autumn: the fruit is harvested and stored, the harvesters give thanks and go on their way.

POSITIVE FORMS

1. **Task Oriented.**
2. **Process-oriented**. The group is ingoing, examining it own psychological process, seeking to understand how it is functioning.
3. **Expressive**. The group is active with celebration and creative expression in word, art, music, song, or movement.
4. **Interactive**. Group members are engaged in interpersonal work and feedback, giving and receiving impressions, sharing attractions and aversions, withdrawing and owning projections.
5. **Confronting**. Members are engaged in creative conflict resolution, in supportive confrontation.
6. **Personal work oriented**. Individual members are taking time for personal growth work. Each one has a turn, working in pairs or small groups, or with you in the presence of the whole group. This work covers a wide

spectrum from cognitive and analytic self-discovery, through emotional disclosure, regression and catharsis.

7. **Charismatic**. The group is attuning to spiritual energies, entering altered states of consciousness and action.

NEGATIVE FORMS

1. **Educational alienation** (confluence). The group is limited to just one kind of learning objective. Its dynamic becomes contracted, cut off from other kinds of being and learning.
2. **Cultural oppression** (liberation). Group behaviour is restricted by oppressive norms, values and beliefs that flow into it and permeate it from the surrounding culture.
3. **Psychological defensiveness** (openness). Group behaviour is distorted by the various anxieties of participants: present and past distress floods the group dynamic, throwing it into rigid, defensive forms, i.e.

Existential and archaic anxieties as a result of primal and present needs.

Acceptance	Will I be accepted, liked, wanted ?
Orientation	Will I be able to understand and be understood ?
Performance	Will I be competent, be able to influence, get what I came for ?
Defensive behaviours	**Submission:** Compulsive dependency, blindly following, seeking permission, shut down, powerless, loss of identity.
	Flight: generalising, theorising, jocularity, gossip, rescue, collusion, etc. insisting on clear task, programme or conventional goal.
	Attack: group leader resisted or proposals rejected etc. criticising, accusing, labelling, stereotyping, invalidating, scapegoating.

Transference: Repressed emotions and feelings are projected on to the group or to an individual member of the group – who is thereby unconsciously appointed to be the current scapegoat for previously experienced psychological hurt and trauma. This blind scapegoating is also a defence against facing and owning and dealing with the hidden pain. A strong projection will not let go of its victim easily, and the deeper the hurt, the more relentless is the projection.

FACILITATION

Facilitation is about helping people to trust one another. Important in this process of growth is creating the right climate for mutual sharing about feelings and attitudes. The 'business' of the church council becomes secondary to the core objective which is about working together, learning together, and achieving together. The leader is part of that process; personal needs such as status, recognition, authority, and expertise, are put aside in the interest of group needs which are related to team cohesion and working together to achieve goals and objectives.

The parish priest as facilitator is a resource person who knows where to go to get what is wanted to achieve the group objective. The facilitator's expertise and skills base will, at this point, be of great value to the group. But it is the group who will provide the power base for directive growth.

If the facilitator feels uncomfortable about this, he or she will need at this point to examine their own agenda. Traditionally, priests have relied upon their historic authority and status to exercise their ministry within a parish, but localised accountability will in future require a more liberating view in which the priest will be expected to exercise a ministry which is reflective of the needs of the community and of the Church. At times the priest as facilitator will need to set aside personal feelings and frustrations and let the church council do things which may not always be comfortable or safe, but the long-term outcome will be a learning experience for all concerned.

The Six Dimensions of Facilitation

1. **Planning**: This is the goal-oriented, ends-and-means, aspect of facilitation: it has to do with the aims of the group, and the programme it should undertake to fulfil them. The facilitative question is: how shall the group acquire its objective and its programme?
2. **Meaning**: This is the cognitive aspect of facilitation: it is related to how participants understand what is going on, and making sense of their experience and knowledge. The facilitative question is: how shall meaning be given to and found in the experiences and actions of group members?
3. **Confronting**: This is the challenge aspect of facilitation: it is about the raising of consciousness, and the group's resistance to and avoidance of the things it needs to face and deal with. The facilitative question is: how shall the group's consciousness be raised about these matters?
4. **Feeling**: This is the affective aspect of facilitation: it has to do with the management of feeling within the group. The facilitative question is: how shall the affective response of members in the group be handled?
5. **Structuring**: This is the formal aspect of facilitation: it is to do with methods of learning, the application of individual experiences within the group, and with how these are to be organised. The facilitative question is: how can the group's learning experiences be structured?
6. **Valuing**: This is the integrity aspect of facilitation: it relates to the creating of a supportive climate which honours and celebrates the personhood of group members – a climate in which group members can be genuine, disclosing their reality as it is, and keeping in touch with their true needs and interests. The facilitative question is: how can such a climate of personal value, integrity and respect be created?

The Three Modes of Facilitation

Hierarchical. Here the facilitator directs the learning process, exercises power over it, and does things for the group, leading from the front by thinking and acting on behalf of the group.

Cooperative. Here the facilitator shares power over the learning process and manages the different dimensions within the group: enabling and guiding the group to become more self-directing in the various forms of learning by conferring with them. The facilitator prompts and helps group members.

Autonomous. Here the facilitator respects the total autonomy of the group: not doing things for them, or with them, but giving them freedom to find their own way, and, without any intervention, exercise their own judgement

Autonomy means a state of being in which each person can, with complete freedom, determine and fulfil their true needs and interests.

Cooperation means mutual aid and support between autonomous persons.

Hierarchy means a state of being in which someone takes responsibility in doing things to or for other persons for the sake of future autonomy and cooperation.

Planning Dimension

Autocratic directive planning. As leader, you make your planning decisions without consulting group members beforehand: you do not first seek their proposals and their evaluations of your ideas. You may seek relevant information prior to devising your plan, such as a list of personal needs and goals.

Without rationale. You present your plan without giving any supporting reasons for it, and its advantages over other alternatives.

With rationale. You present your plan and give supporting reasons and stress its advantages.

Facilitator-centred negotiated planning. As leader, you first propose your version of the parish programme then invite group members to propose their modifications of it, and negotiate with them until the final version is agreed. This can be preceded by council members writing out lists of personal needs. It is best to reach a decision by a consensus decision-making procedure, as defined below.

Strong form. You present a fully detailed programme for the group to consider and negotiate on.

Weak form. You give only broad outlines of a programme, modify and agree on this, then work with the council to fill it in.

Contractually delegated group planning. As leader, you define with the council, by direction or negotiation, a whole block of learning in terms of its main objectives and the overall time to be taken for it; or in terms of some broad parameters. Within this outline contract, all planning is undertaken by council members on their own: they decide who does what and how they work together.

The Confronting Dimension

Confronting interpretation. As facilitator, you interrupt the resistant behaviour – of one or some or all of the group – and identify it as a way of not dealing with some issue. This is done in a manner that is supportive of the persons concerned.

Confrontation action. When confronting one or more persons, or the group as a whole, you propose an action – doing or saying something – that challenges and interrupts the defensive behaviour in those concerned.

Inviting a confronting interpretation. When some or all of the group are resistant and blocked, you invite those concerned to come forward with their own account of the threatening issue, or of the avoidance behaviour, or of the source of this behaviour, or of some combination of these. You then ask for the views of others. You may then add your own view as one among many.

Confronting questions. This is a more head-on technique. You can put a straight, direct question that interrupts the resistant behaviour, and ask those concerned to raise their own consciousness about it.

Descriptive confrontation. You simply make a descriptive comment about the avoidance behaviour, without attaching any kind of interpretation to it, or without asking anyone to interpret it, i.e. 'You have just spent 20 minutes criticising the parish hall.'

Structured self-confrontation. You set up an exercise in which each person takes it in turn, in small groups to confront themselves about what issues they are currently avoiding, how they are avoiding them, and what the source of the avoidance seems to be.

COUNSELLING

Counselling is a skill for which you need considerable training, support, and practice; and also one where it is possible to do harm with well-meant, but clumsy interventions. However, the basic skills are within any competent parson's reach. If at any point you feel out of your depth in offering counselling, you should realise your limitations and seek more skilled help for the person you are trying to counsel.

The Difference Between Counselling and Advising

Counselling aims to help people to help themselves by working through their problems – for example, by viewing them from different angles and by identifying possible solutions. In this way, people can come to *their own* informed decisions. The counsellor prompts, asks questions, but does not offer an opinion of his or her own, or make judgmental comments. This is completely different from when you are advising someone, for then you do recommend a suitable course of action in a directive way, using phrases such as:

'You should......',
'I think the best way forward is',
'I would suggest that',

For personal issues, where it is important that people take responsibility for their own problems, counselling is more effective than advising. Internal stress caused by someone's attitudes or reactions to a situation can *only* be resolved by that person, *not* by you.

Deciding on the Extent of Your Counselling Role

Before starting to counsel someone about a problem, you first need to clarify your role. At one end of the spectrum, this may be to help someone to talk to a more appropriate counsellor; in the middle it may be to carry out some initial counselling; and at the other end of the spectrum it may be to carry out a full, confidential, counselling process.

Whatever you feel is most appropriate will depend on your confidence in your own skills, the nature of the problem, and the other resources available (for instance, a spiritual director, or specialist agency, e.g. AA).

Counselling Skills

Overall, the role of the counsellor is that of a facilitator rather than an implementor. You focus on *someone else's* problems, feelings, and views, while often (though not always) keeping your *own* to yourself.

Many of the skills involved are at odds with the everyday tasks of parochial care, such as putting over your own views, making decisions, using a directive approach, making judgments, criticisms and evaluations. So you may need to adjust some of your normal ways of behaving and reacting.

The key skills you need to develop are:

- the ability to focus attention on other people
- listening
- showing that you are listening
- empathy
- using questions effectively to encourage talking and to probe aspects of the problem
- reading and using body language
- being non-judgmental
- feeling and showing an interest in other people's problems
- keeping an open mind
- being able to see a situation from someone else's point of view
- helping people to explore their problems
- helping to identify solutions

● helping to work out the implications of different decisions
● remaining objective

Listening to or 'attending' in a Counselling Context

Listening – or 'attending' – in a counselling context means giving your *FULL* attention. This is in contrast to a meeting, where you are often working out other people's reactions, and assessing whether everything is going your way when you listen to what someone else is saying.

Listening is not a *passive* process, because as well as absorbing what someone is saying, you need to let the other person know in some *active* way that you have heard and understood.

The person you intend to help may think you do not really understand what he or she is saying. You can show that you have heard and understood by using '*REFLECTING SKILLS*' whereby you 'reflect back' what he or she has been saying. This is likely to take the form of paraphrasing, or summarising the main points made.

For example:
Incumbent: 'I've not really been myself lately, what with the change to a new parish, all the moving and the upset ....and I've been getting these splitting headaches since the move. It's all a bit much ....'
Counsellor: 'Mmm, you feel overwhelmed by the move, and you've been getting headaches ....'

You can also show that you are listening by using body language, such as nodding, or saying quietly, 'mmm', or 'aha', as your staff member is talking.

Being Non-judgmental

This means accepting what someone says, without passing judgment on it, or evaluating it. It means setting aside your own feelings, and focusing only on the other person's experience.

If the counsellor in the above example had said 'so, you think change is a problem', the counsellor would have been interpreting the situation to someone who may not think change is a problem at all – and would have moved the conversation *away* from that person's experience.

Using Questions in a Counselling Context

If the counsellor had said to the incumbent in the above example, 'Did the headaches start at the time of the move?' The reply would probably have been 'yes' or 'no'. This is an example of a closed question, which gains specific information, but is unlikely to encourage the incumbent to keep talking.

Closed questions may be helpful in the later stages of the counselling process; but initially, *open* questions, which encourage the person seeking counselling to talk, are more helpful. Open questions often start with 'how?', 'what?', 'where?', and 'why?'.

For example, 'When did your headaches start?'.

Multiple questions (i.e., two or more questions in one) are to be avoided at all costs.

For example, 'When you moved to your new job, why did you opt to dispense with the services of your Reader, was it because you felt threatened?'

This is a double question, and would be confusing to answer.

Body Language

Body language is important in *all* interpersonal communication, but it is *especially* so if you are counselling someone.

For example, if someone seeking counselling is sitting with legs crossed, with one arm across the chest, one hand supporting the head, and leaning a lot to one side, you might infer a degree of insecurity and defensiveness.

The counsellor needs to project a relaxed, available image, which can be achieved through an open, comfortable posture, with relaxed shoulders, the body upright, and hands on one's lap.

Anger is often expressed through raised shoulders, leaning forward, tense facial expression and louder and more highly pitched speech. Someone who is upset may be quiet and withdrawn, and avoid eye contact.

Feelings of depression may be expressed through slow movements, a serious expression, and hunched posture.

Happiness may be expressed through smiling (which can be seen in the eyes as well as the mouth).

Feelings of tension are reflected through tense muscles, possibly in the forehead, round the mouth, in the jaw, hands, shoulders etc.

Impatience is often reflected in repetitive movements such as finger-tapping, foot-tapping, looking at a watch etc.

Useful Counselling Prompts

'Stuck' sessions can be 'moved-on' using the following phrases:

summarising 'So, the main points we've talked about are.......'

open questions 'Can you tell me a bit more about ...?'

active listening 'You seem to feel .... because .... and what you want (or need) is....

paraphrasing 'Let me see if I understand you – what you've been saying is .....

probing 'Can you give me an example?'

confronting 'On the one hand you .... but on the other hand ....

alternative frameworks 'Viewed differently, it could be that ....'

checking interpretations 'It seems to me that .... is that how it seems to you?'

focusing 'What seems important is ....'

interpreting 'It seems implicit in what you're saying that....'

clarifying 'I'm not sure I understand. Can you tell me a bit more (or again) about ....'

divergent thinking 'Let's examine some ways in which you could get answers to those questions ....'

Phrases to Avoid – 'You should / must / ought .... What I would do is .... Pull yourself together. You are quite wrong How on earth can you say that? You are no different from anyone else around here ....'

The Four Stages of Counselling

Counselling works through four stages:

1) Starting to talk
2) Exploring the problem
3) Clarifying the situation, and generating solutions
4) Choosing and implementing a solution

Depending on the complexity of the problem, these stages may be dealt with in one meeting, or spread out over a number of meetings.

You may have decided, when you defined the extent of your helping role, that you want to restrict your involvement, in which case you need only to work through the relevant stages.

1) Starting to Talk

This is potentially the most difficult stage, because if it goes wrong, there may be no way to restart the process.

It is usually easier to get started if someone has made an initial approach to you, than if you have to make the initial approach.

The first step will be to find a private place where you will not be interrupted.

The next step may be to rearrange the seating. Sitting in comfortable chairs around two adjacent sides of a table is less threatening than sitting on opposite sides. Even better is not **to have a table at all**.

The confidentiality of the meeting needs to be made clear, by saying, for example that nothing will be repeated.

You will need to decide how to start the conversation; you could try 'Bob, I've noticed that you haven't been so cheerful recently, and I wonder if you would like to talk about it?'

Assuming your colleague agrees, you should encourage him to do most of the talking at this stage, by using your listening skills. Reflect and summarise to show that you hear what is being said, and use open questions to encourage talking. AVOID EVALUATING OR JUDGING

The overall aim of this stage is to decide whether there is a difficulty you can help with, and whether you both want to discuss the matter further. If the incumbent or assistant priest does *not* want to, there is little you can do except make it clear that you are still available if there is a change of heart.

2) Exploring the Problem

This stage may run straight on from the previous one, or may be a separate meeting. The aim is to help someone explore the problem fully. You will need to use all the key counselling skills, with plenty of open questions to get the picture, and probing questions to fill any gaps.

You may need to give your colleague permission to speak freely. Phrases like, 'I shouldn't complain', should be followed by your saying 'It's OK to complain if you want to'.

You may also need to decipher the individual's codes. For example, 'I don't care' may mean 'I'm trying hard not to care'.

Be prepared for emotional outbursts – such as crying or shaking which are natural ways of releasing tension. If this happens, just remain calm and reassure the individual that it's OK to cry here.

Be prepared for long silences – and *do not* rush to fill them.

Afterwards, you may want to make a note of the emerging problem(s).

3) Interpreting the Situation and Generating Solutions

In this stage, the aim is to help a colleague to understand better the situation he or she is in, and why he or she feels threatened by it. BEWARE OF THE ATTITUDE THAT YOU ARE THERE TO GIVE ALL THE ANSWERS. Your role is to encourage *your colleague* **to take responsibility** for *managing* the pressure, while confirming that you are there to help.

This is the stage at which you are most likely to use 'Challenging' or 'Confronting' **interventions**.

For example: 'You've said a lot about how irritating you find your son's behaviour. Are there any aspects of your own behaviour that you think might be encouraging him to behave in this way?'

Or you might want to ask what the ideal solution is, and then ask: 'What's standing in your way?'

Encourage the idea of making choices, however small. For example: 'You say you were brought up in care so you never had a chance; but that still leaves you with plenty of choice over what you decide now. What are your choices in this situation?'

'Brainstorming' is a useful technique to use for creating solutions where none are forthcoming.

4) Choosing and Implementing a Solution

The main point here is that it is *Your colleague* who has to live with the chosen solution. This may be quite a different decision from the one you would make. But the choice is *not* yours.

Counsellors who work in a structured way often have a battery of resources available for this stage (forms for decision-making, goal-setting, action-planning etc.).

In the absence of these instruments, it is useful to bring to the mind of the person you are working with the following criteria for evaluating the proposed solutions:

Do you have everything you need to carry out the proposed solution?

Is it relevant to solving the problem?

Is it in keeping with your values?

Are there any major obstacles in the way of carrying it out?

This stage should conclude with specific goals and targets set; and (possibly) with a further meeting arranged to review the counsellee's progress.

And finally look after yourself

You may find that someone is troubled by a fairly minor point, such as poor communication, and the whole issue can be resolved in a half-hour talk followed by the implementation of a communication strategy.

On the other hand, the problem may be complex, including, for example, a sick relative, an unsatisfactory relationship with a parishioner, or low self-esteem. This may take weeks to unravel, and your colleague may become dependent on you. In this case, you can look after yourself by limiting the frequency of meetings – say, to one a week, finding someone to act as your supervisor – someone you can discuss the 'case' with in confidence, so that *You* do not become stressed by other people's problems.

Crisis care

Those who have the care and responsibility for others must also have the ability to respond appropriately to the cry for help which follows upon a personal tragedy, such as the loss of a loved one, or the bewilderment and sense of total inadequacy which follows upon involvement in a life-threatening incident or trauma such as a major disaster.

What is termed 'Psychological' de-briefing, as part of a proactive intervention programme, can reduce dramatically the emotional and physical reactions experienced by clergy and others who are exposed to traumatic incidents. Research has indicated that stress reactions following a traumatic incident can be reduced by up to 80% by the implementation of a support strategy which includes a review of thoughts, feelings, actions, and reactions, if undertaken within 72 hours.

Psychological trauma is mostly caused by lack of understanding about reactions, isolation from colleagues, family and friends, a sense of lack of control, and a fear about the future. The aim of the de-brief is to allow traumatised clergy to share impressions, feelings and reactions with others; and to describe their role and activity during and after the crisis incident. The de-briefing programme has seven distinct stages:-

Initial stage

In this first stage the objective is to motivate the participant to talk about the trauma and to set the ground rules. The issue of confidentiality is emphasised, and participants are encouraged to take their time, and are assured that you are there to help them.

Establishing the Facts

The participant is asked to describe what his or her role was in the incident and what happened. A brief synopsis of the crisis event will usually suffice.

Thought Stage

At the thought stage, the task is to get participants to discuss the first or most prominent thoughts which entered their minds during the incident. This is frequently the first time he or she may have had the opportunity to personalise their experience by expressing personal thoughts on what happened and why.

Reaction Stage

This is probably the most emotionally powerful part of crisis care when people are asked 'what was the worst thing about the incident for you personally?'. Discussion may move slowly or rapidly depending on the nature of the incident. Ample time is allowed to discuss the most traumatic aspect of the crisis. Anger, fear, frustration, grief, loss, emptiness, guilt and other emotional responses are very common reactions; and emotional outbursts are accepted as valid and expected under the circumstances.

Symptom Stage

The signs and symptoms stage provides the carer with an indi-cation of the degree of emotional and psychophysical response at each stage of the trauma. This stage is particularly important as a mechanism by which the carer can determine the need for follow up services.

Preparation Stage

This stage is an important opportunity for the carer to pass on stress survival skills. Many practical suggestions are given at this stage and individuals are encouraged to continue to take appropriate steps to manage their stress in the days which follow.

Re-Entry Stage

During the re-entry stage, future planning and coping are discussed. One of the main aims at this point in the crisis care programme, is to underline the support which clergy can expect to receive from the Church at times of crisis, to review what has been disclosed, to summarise comments, to encourage, and to offer further assistance, and tie up the loose ends.

DEPRESSION

Everyone feels fed up and miserable at times, and usually the reason seems obvious, but not always, sometimes we are in a mood – and we really don't know why. We are all prone to bouts of depression but for some of us it can be so severe that it dominates our lives, making it barely worth living. It just does not help to say 'pull yourself together.' The kind of depression I refer to is that which makes you feel hopeless about recovery and which, for a period of months or years, makes it impossible for you to carry on at work, and might mean that you change your life pattern and your kind of job. Depression of this magnitude is an illness and needs treatment.

A characteristic of depression appears to be that sufferers feel that others cannot possibly understand what it is really like.

Depression should be viewed more broadly; it is a social, educational, economic, moral and ethical problem, as well as a challenge to medicine.

The onset of depression can be a responsive reaction to bereavement, stress, overwork, unrealistic goal-setting, unemployment, money problems, housing, or simply ill-health (e.g. M.E.).

While much is known about depression, much still needs to be learned about its prime causes

Principal reactive causes

TRAUMATIC EVENT
PERCEIVED LACK OF SUPPORT/CONCERN/LOVE
PHYSICAL ILLNESS
PERSONALITY – EARLY EXPERIENCES
WORK -

It is frequently said that work is a great safeguard against depression. Some types of work, however, can be causative, especially work which is either stressful and over-demanding, or which makes no demands upon our intellect or ability because it is uninteresting and unchallenging.

People who are unemployed, retired, or who suffer from enforced idleness through physical disability, are also liable to depression. To feel unwanted, useless, and a drag on others, is psychologically damaging to self-esteem and self-worth.

Aiming at unrealistically high standards can also sow the seeds of anxiety and depression; the antidote to this is knowing ourselves, our strengths and weaknesses, our powers and limitations, and our potential – both mental, and physical.

Symptoms of Depression

- LOSS OF INTEREST AND ENJOYMENT IN LIFE
- A LACK OF DRIVE AND MOTIVATION
- AGITATION
- RESTLESSNESS
- LOSS OF APPETITE
- SLEEPLESSNESS
- GOING OFF SEX
- FEELING USELESS, INADEQUATE, HELPLESS
- LOSS OF SELF-CONFIDENCE
- IRRITABILITY
- THOUGHTS OF SUICIDE

About one in ten people who suffer from serious depression will also have periods when they are elated and overactive. This form of depression is known as manic-depression.

Anxiety and Depression

There are important differences between anxiety and depression, namely:-

Thought content of anxiety and depression in relation to Beck's cognitive triad of self, world and future:

Anxiety	**Depression**
View of self as vulnerable 'Something awful is about to happen.'	View of self as negative 'I am a failure.'
View of world as threatening 'You cannot trust anybody.'	View of world as negative 'It's just one catastrophe after another.'
View of future as unpredictable 'I have to keep on guard, anything could happen.'	View of future as negative 'It's hopeless, there's nothing to look forward to.'

Typical feelings, behaviours and reactions associated with anxiety and depression:

	ANXIETY	DEPRESSION
FEELINGS	Apprehension	Sadness
BEHAVIOURS	Avoidance	Procrastination
	Excessive	Indecisiveness
	dependency	Impaired concentration
REACTIONS	Tension	Difficulty getting to
	Palpitations	sleep. Early morning
		awakening

Treatment

a) Medical

Antidepressants – their action is slow and long-term, and there may be side-effects – e.g. dry mouth , constipation, drowsiness.

b) Psychological

Seeking help, which may take the form of talking things through with a friend, a trained counsellor, or psychologist/ psychoanalyst

c) Self-help

A very important aspect of recovery from depression is to increase the number and scope of pleasurable experiences. Seeking out activities and situations that provide the necessary uplift and have a proven therapeutic value. Treatments focussing on interpersonal skills, cognitions, or activity schedules (increasing the number and frequency of pleasant activities and keeping a daily diary of them) have all significantly alleviated depression.

THE HASSLE FACTOR

Stress research has tended in the past to concentrate on dramatic life events as the probable cause or precursor to stress related illness. Recent studies, however, have thrown a

The major obstacles to full recovery are:-

(1) Denial that a problem exists
(2) Evasion of the problem (e.g.,via alcohol)
(3) Refusal to seek or accept help
(4) Inability to express or master negative feelings
(5) Failure to explore possible causes
(6) Failure to explore alternative solutions
(7) Projection on to others of total responsibility for causing/curing crisis
(8) Turning away from family and friends

To overcome depression you should
ask yourself these questions:-

1. Do I want to get rid of my depression?
2. Am I using depression as an excuse, or as protection?
3. Have I decided that I can and will recover?
4. Do I have faith in myself?
5. Am I getting to know myself better?
6. Am I planning and acting to improve my self-image?
7. Do I really know my strengths and weaknesses?
8. Will I spare for myself a little of the love and forgiveness, I feel and now pledge myself to develop for others?

spotlight on the effect of relatively minor, but more frequent daily events on stress levels. Those irritating, frustrating, or distressing incidents that occur in everyday life which range from getting stuck in a traffic jam, losing a wallet or a bunch of keys, to having an argument with a teenage son or daughter, or a clash of opinion with a colleague at work, may be more closely linked to and may have as great an effect on our moods and our health as the major catastrophes which strike each one of us from time to time.

Lazarus (1981)* and Taylor (1986)* found that the more

*Lazarus, R.S. (1981) Little hassles can be hazardous to health: *Psychology Today*, July 1981
*Taylor, S.E. (1986) *Health Psychology*: Random House, New York

frequent and intense the 'hassles' people reported, the poorer their overall mental and physical health. This finding has an important bearing on stress management as a possible indicator of your own current stress level, or that of a colleague.

The impact of minor irritating events on our health and well-being depends upon their frequency, duration and intensity. Likewise our response to a given 'hassle', is related closely to other factors such as personality, coping style, and how the rest of our day has gone. When under pressure we are also prone to react more strongly to those little things that go wrong. Lazarus suspects that some of the impact of hassles may stem from their personal meaning and significance, but equally they may be related to our ineptness in coping with certain inter-personal difficulties.

Lazarus drew attention to the fact that 'psychological stress resides neither in the situation nor the person; it depends on a transaction between the two. It arises from how the person appraises an event and adapts to it'. What makes a situation more stressful to one person and not to another is determined by the accumulative effect of previous events and life experiences, in conjunction with temperament, feelings, current health, age, and the presence or absence of support from others. There is usually some 'last straw' which is the precipitating factor in making the stress unbearable; it is important therefore to recognise this last straw as the occasion for the crisis and not the cause.

Uplifts, those pleasant, happy, or satisfying experiences like hearing good news, getting a good night's sleep, or solving a difficult problem, may serve as breathers, sustainers or restorers when psychological resources have been drained during periods of stress. Psychologists have discovered that the uplifts of everyday life can actually buffer people against stress induced illness The joy and happiness we experience when we are with the people we cherish most, having a meal with friends, listening to a favourite piece of music, feeling relaxed and in a holiday mood, help us to restore inner resources, and provide a respite, sanctuary, and breathing space from the stresses of life. The uplifts can be seen as high ground from which we can confront and overcome the worst effects of worry and anxiety.

Consistent with this line of research Cohen and Hoberman (1983)* found that positive life events ameliorated psychological distress and physical symptoms for people under high degrees of stress. What are the ten most common sources of pleasures and hassles in life? When Lazarus and his colleagues asked a group of 100 middle-class, middle-aged men and women in the U.S.A. to record their hassles and uplifts over a a one-year period, their answers were, in order of frequency:-

Hassles

1. Concern about weight
2. Health of a family member
3. Rising prices of common goods
4. Home maintenance
5. Too many things to do
6. Misplacing or losing things
7. Outside maintenance
8. Property, investment, taxes
9. Crime
10. Physical appearance

Uplifts

1. Relating well with a spouse or lover
2. Relating well with friends
3. Completing a task
4. Feeling healthy
5. Getting enough sleep
6. Eating out
7. Meeting responsibilities
8. Visiting, phoning, or writing to someone
9. Spending time with one's family
10. A pleasing home

* Cohens, S. & Hoberman, H.M. (1983) Positive events and social supports as buffers of life change stress. 13. 99-125.

Chapter Five

Coping Resources

COPING WITH STRESS

By identifying, describing, and classifying specific strategies which clergy employ in coping with work stress, old ideas can be challenged and fresh insights encouraged in an endeavour to reduce the level of stress currently experienced by clergy in their work role.

How ministers 'cope' with potentially stressful situations in their ministry is dependent upon the adoption of an effective coping strategy.

In Dewe's Study (1987)* of Protestant clergy in New Zealand, ministers were asked to think of a time when they felt under stress and to 'describe the sorts of things which caused stress'. The responses were grouped under six headings which included:-

a) Work overload – too many meetings to the detriment of pastoral work; time pressures.
b) Role conflicts – balancing family and work priorities; conflicts between planned and crisis work; church conservatism.
c) Role ambiguity – uncertainty of job tenure; uncertainty surrounding church issues – church union.
d) Dealing with grief and people in need – death of a parishioner; troubled people who need constant help; welfare work.

*Dewe, P.J. (1987). New Zealand Ministers of Religion:Identifying sources of stress and coping strategies. *Work & Stress* 1.4. 351-362

e) Relationships with parishioners and parish – unrealistic demands of parish; motivating parishioners; lack of finances for parish.

f) Self pressures – inability to say 'no'; not appreciating one's own limitations; difficulties in delegating.

To find out how clergy coped, Dewe asked the clergy participants in his study to think of a time when they felt under 'stress', and then explain how they managed to cope with it. 73 coping actions were described, and, distinguishing between direct action (problem solving) strategies and palliative strategies (reducing the feelings of emotional discomfort), it was possible to classify 33% of the responses as direct actions (for example keeping committee work to a minimum; do one thing at a time; work out a systematic plan) and 67% as palliatives (for example share with prayer group; quiet time every day; do what can be done and forget the rest; make use of hobbies-leisure).

Following upon his initial study, Dewe went on to design and distribute a questionnaire which was sent to all ministers of the Protestant Church in New Zealand. Analysis of the data returns (60%), revealed three principal work stress factors, namely:-

1. Parish conflicts and church conservatism which included conflicts between the minister and the parish-parishioners, first in terms of expectations (for example other people not accepting what you are) and second in terms of attitudes and values (for example dealing with prejudice in others), conflicts between the church's teaching and personal beliefs (for example being asked to make statements on questions you have not yet personally resolved), conflicts with church conservatism (for example the feeling that you are continually propping up a cumbersome institutional structure), and conflict over administrative issues (for example other people not meeting deadlines).

2. Difficulties involving parish commitment and development, for example, the reluctance of parishioners to grow, self development issues (the feelings of inadequacy through inability to meet the full pastoral needs of the people), and contact-isolation concerns (for example, too little time to get to know people).

3. Emotional and time difficulties surrounding crisis work which includes administrative difficulties – never being able to work to a set routine: someone always wanting something at inconvenient times, emotional demands – dealing with people in desperate need, and time concerns – necessary and important tasks being overshadowed because administrative duties have to be carried out.

In a component analysis of some 65 coping strategies Dewe highlighted five factors accounting for 33% of the data variance.

a) Social Support, which included 'talking it through' with someone else, getting advice-help-suggestions from others, and releasing emotion and irritation by 'letting off steam' to colleagues.

b) Postponing action by relaxation and distraction, which may take the form of (i) distracting yourself by engaging in fun-leisure activities, (ii) avoiding-ignoring the problem, and (iii) simply dropping what you are doing and take up something totally unrelated.

c) Developing a capacity to deal with the problem, which includes strategies for pacing yourself by leaving margins of time between activities, strategies for conserving energy, e.g. not working so hard, strategies designed to enhance one's capacity, taking exercise to reduce tension, strategies which identify personal limitations, and strategies which include seeing the humorous aspects of a situation.

d) Rationalising the problem by (1) putting things into perspective, accepting the situation, and getting on with it, (2), clarifying-explaining your position and letting others know where you stand, and (3), using work itself as the means for rationalising work behaviour, e.g. working harder and longer.

e) Support through spiritual commitment, through prayer, family loyalty, solitude, a 'quiet time' each day, and through self-reappraisal.

Dewe's study draws attention to the important role palliatives (emotion-focussed) coping strategies have for ministers which implies that many of the stressors related to the occupational environment cannot be resolved by 'problem-focussed' strategies. Dewe states that there may be little, if anything, many ministers can do to deal directly with certain stressors, thus, strategies which allow for the dissipation or regulation of emotional discomfort should be regarded as a legitimate part of coping and an important aspect of our coping repertoire.

COPING TASKS:

Coping should be thought of not only as a set of processes which occur in reaction to the problems posed by a particular stressor, but also as efforts aimed at achieving certain goals.

Coping efforts centre on five main tasks:......

1. to reduce harmful environmental conditions and enhance prospects of recovery
2. to tolerate or adjust to negative events or realities
3. to maintain a positive self-image
4. to maintain emotional equilibrium
5. to continue satisfying relationships with others.

COPING RESOURCES

- Try to keep things in perspective
- Try to avoid confrontation
- Try to relax after work
- Try to take some immediate action on the basis of your present understanding of the situation
- Think objectively about the situation and keep your feelings under control
- Stand back and rationalise the situation
- Try to nip potential sources of stress in the bud
- Try to reassure yourself everything is going to work out alright
- Do not let the problem go until you have solved it or reconciled it satisfactorily
- Make sure people are aware that you are doing your best
- Try to forget work when the workday is finished

- Try to see the humour of the situation
- Consider a range of alternatives for handling sources of stress
- Set priorities
- Make a concerted effort to enjoy yourself with some pleasurable activity after work
- Try not to overdwell on problems
- Share your feelings and frustrations with others
- Think of good things for the future
- Talk through the situation/problem with someone at work

A COPING CHECKLIST

The coping checklist below is designed to provide you with an indication of how well you are coping with your job. Circle the number which most nearly fits you.

1 = very true
2 = quite true
3 = somewhat true
4 = not very true
5 = not at all true

1. Setting priorities and dealing with problems accordingly	1 2 3 4 5
2. Concentrating on specific problems	1 2 3 4 5
3. Managing time effectively	1 2 3 4 5
4. Planning ahead	1 2 3 4 5
5. Dealing with situations objectively	1 2 3 4 5
6. Seeking stable relationships	1 2 3 4 5
7. Having interests and activities outside work	1 2 3 4 5
8. Having hobbies and pastimes	1 2 3 4 5
9. Not using distractions to take my mind off things	1 2 3 4 5
10. Deliberately separating Home and Work	1 2 3 4 5
11. Talking to understanding friends	1 2 3 4 5
12. Seeking as much social support as possible	1 2 3 4 5
13. Not 'bottling things up'	1 2 3 4 5
14. Seeking support and advice from superiors	1 2 3 4 5
15. Not 'Putting things off'	1 2 3 4 5
16. Dealing with problems immediately	1 2 3 4 5

17. Reorganising work   1 2 3 4 5
18. Looking for ways to make work interesting   1 2 3 4 5
19. Having a home that is a refuge   1 2 3 4 5
20. Keeping emotions in check   1 2 3 4 5
21. Keeping busy   1 2 3 4 5
22. Recognising limitations   1 2 3 4 5
23. Not avoiding situations   1 2 3 4 5
24. Accepting situations and learning to live
    with them   1 2 3 4 5
25. Not hiding behind rules and regulations   1 2 3 4 5
26. Delegating wherever possible   1 2 3 4 5

Scoring Directions: Add together the numbers you circled for the questions contained in each of the eight coping scales.

Prioritising/objective coping	1 – 7	Score............
Utilising hobbies and leisure time	8 – 10	Score............
Mobilising social support	11 – 14	Score............
Time measures	15 – 16	Score............
Innovations	17 – 18	Score............
Suppression of stress	19 – 21	Score............
Non-confrontation	22 – 24	Score............
Non-involvement	25 – 26	Score............

The overall total score can range between 26 and 130. Scores of 78 or more may suggest some general difficulty in coping with the dimensions covered.

Coping with a Personal Crisis

A personal crisis shows up human weaknesses as well as strengths. The feelings and emotions which may be experienced range from, helplessness, and sadness, to guilt, shame, anger, and disappointment.

The above affect measure will help you to determine the nature and intensity of your reactions following a personal crisis. It can also be used in counselling a colleague or parishioner who has come to you for help and guidance, following a personal tragedy.

The mind has its own 'safety valve' which enables us to minimise the effect of trauma by allowing the misfortune to be

Stress Event Affect Measure

Look at the statements below. If you have had the similar thoughts and feelings following a recent stressful incident please indicate whether 'rarely', 'sometimes', 'often'. or 'not at all', in the appropriate column by a tick (/)

	not at all 0	rarely 1	sometimes 2	often 3
1 I think about it when I try not to				
2 I try not to get upset about it				
3 I try not to think about it				
4 I have trouble getting to sleep				
5 I feel angry and upset about it				
6 I dream about it				
7 I try not to be reminded of it				
8 I try to pretend it has not happened				
9 I try not to talk about it				
10 I keep picturing it in my mind				
11 Other things keep reminding me of it				
12 I try not to dwell on it				
13 I get angry when I am reminded of it				
14 I feel numbed by it				
15 I keep feeling it is going to happen to me				

felt only gradually. At first a numbness may be experienced which may give the event the semblance of a dream, 'it hasn't really happened'. This may seem to others to be a sign that you do not care, or are being very strong. As you allow the trauma more into your conscious mind there is a need to face it, to think about it, and to talk to someone about it. At this stage you should try to seek out someone who will listen sympathetically to you, someone who will understand; someone, perhaps who has gone through a similar experience and from whom you can receive practical and emotional support.

To cope with their feelings, some people require 'space' and privacy; they need to be left alone. Knowing when to stay and when to leave is a skill which comes from observing and taking one's cues from body language.

When to seek help

1. If you feel tense, confused, empty or exhausted,
2. If, after a month, you continue to feel numb or need to keep busy and active to stop you thinking,
3. If, you continue to have nightmares and sleep badly,
4. If you want to share your feelings with others and cannot,
5. If your relationships appear to be suffering,
6. If you have become more prone to accidents,
7. If you smoke or drink to excess, or take drugs,
8. If your work suffers.

Help is at hand from your GP, Cruse, the Samaritans, A.A., and Specialist Support Groups – people who care about you!

Chapter Six

Managing Personal Stress

STRESS REACTIONS

Stress reactions to the pressures of parochial ministry can be grouped into three main categories which relate to how we feel about ourselves, how we feel about other people, and the way in which our bodies react to stress build-up.

Stress Reaction Checklist

A. How we feel about ourselves
1. Oversensitivity to criticism
2. Feelings of insecurity
3. Lack of confidence
4. Guilt
5. Anger
6. Frustration
7. Depression
8. Hopelessness
9. Indecisiveness
10. Sense of inadequacy
B. How we feel about other people
1. Anger
2. Irritability
3. Intolerance
4. Lack of sympathy and understanding
C. Physical reactions to stress
1. Exhaustion
2. Headaches
3. Tension

4. Sleeplessness
5. Helplessness
6. Recurrent illness

Dunham's research* indicates that when coping strategies are ineffective and personal resources have become depleted, the likely sequence of events is, first a feeling of panic and a sense of urgency which will make itself felt by an overwhelming desire to get things done at the double – including eating and drinking, and our current workload. The second stage is marked by increasing irritability , over-reaction, frustration, memory loss, and altered sleep patterns. The third stage is where the brain takes over by going into survival mode (see Chapter One). At this point you are likely to experience the following autonomic symptoms.

1. Palpitations and chest pains
2. Panic feelings
3. Lowered resistance to virus infections etc.
4. Loss of concentration
5. Difficulty in remembering things
6. Heightened emotion (being close to tears)
7. Sadness and depression
8. Loss of interest in life

Burnout is the name frequently used in describing the point where we have become, through pressures of work, exhausted both mentally and physically.

The diagram on the next page shows the relationship between work pressure, performance, and what happens when we fail to pace ourselves.

ARE YOU A WORKAHOLIC

A Workaholic is a person whose work has become the dominant factor in life, to the extent that it tends to interfere with other aspects of social activity and interpersonal behaviour.

The following questions are designed to identify those who may be concerned that their work is becoming all-

*Dunham, J, (1992) Stress in Teaching. Routledge: London

WHERE ARE YOU ON THE PRESSURE/PERFORMANCE GRAPH?

As pressures (Stressors) increase so does performance
– up to a point

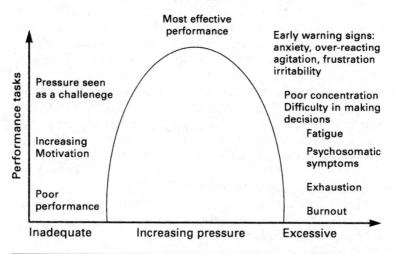

Most effective
performance

Early warning signs:
anxiety, over-reacting
agitation, frustration
irritability

Poor concentration
Difficulty in making
decisions

Fatigue

Psychosomatic
symptoms

Exhaustion

Burnout

Pressure seen
as a challenege

Increasing
Motivation

Poor
performance

Performance tasks

Inadequate   Increasing pressure   Excessive

Plot where you are now and where you would like to be

YOU CAN BE IN THE MOST EFFECTIVE PERFORMANCE
AREA ALL THE TIME BY STUDYING THE FACT SHEETS
AND FOLLOWING THE ACTION PLANS

encompassing, and who think that now is the time to take
stock and to redress balances.

If the instructions are followed correctly the resultant score
will tell you:

a) whether you should re-evaluate the dominance of work in
    your life, and,
b) whether you are striking a happy balance between work
    and other activities in your life.

Those who have a healthy attitude to work and its place in
their lives may give the same answers as those who are
obsessed with work, but the out-and-out workaholic will probably answer nearly all of them as indicated opposite:

(1) Yes (2) Yes (3) Yes (4) yes (5) Yes (6) Yes (7) Yes (8) No
(9) Yes (10) Yes) (11) Yes (12) Yes (13) No (14) Yes (15) Yes
(16) Yes (17) Yes (18) Yes (19) Yes (20) Yes (21) Yes (22) Yes

ARE YOU A WORKAHOLIC?

1. Do you seem to communicate better with your co-workers than with your spouse (or best friend)?
2. Are you always punctual for appointments?
3. Are you better able to relax on your days off than on Saturday afternoons(work anticipation!)
4. Are you more comfortable when you are productive than idle?
5. Do you carefully organise your hobbies?
6. Are you usually very annoyed when your spouse/friend keeps you waiting?
7. Are most recreational activities with work colleagues?
8. Does your spouse/friend think of you as an easy-going person?
9. If you play tennis or squash do you occasionally see (or want to see) your least-liked person's face on the ball before a smash?
10. Do you tend to substitute your work for interpersonal contacts; that is, is work sometimes a way of avoiding close relationships?
11. Even under pressure, do you usually take the extra time to make sure you have all the facts before making a decision?
12. Do you usually plan every step of the itinerary of a trip in advance and tend to become uncomfortable if plans go awry?
13. Do you enjoy small talk at a reception or cocktail party?
14. Are most of your friends clergy colleagues?
15. Do you still carry on working when you are sick?
16. Is most of your reading work-related?
17. Do you work on when others have stopped?
18. Do you talk of parish matters on social occasions?
19. Do you wake up in the night worrying about the parish/parishioners?
20. Do your dreams tend to centre on parish conflicts?
21. Do you play as hard as you work?
22. Do you tend to become restless on holidays?

If you have answered YES to most of the above, YOU ARE A WORKAHOLIC

Talking through your answers to the above questions with a colleague will help you to put your work role into perspective in relation to other aspects of your life.

SELF-INFLICTED STRESSORS

After studying the Stressors listed below, ask yourself:-
   Which of these are self inflicted?
   Which can be lessened?

Stressors in Ministry

1. ORGANISATIONAL
   a) Hierarchy remote and impersonal.
   b) Lack of support from above.
   c) Ineffective leadership.
   d) Lack of consultation on major issues.
   e) Ineffective communication system.
   f) Increasing bureaucracy.
   g) Increase in the number of non-parochial appointments.
   h) Too many changes too quickly.
   i) Synodical government remote from grass-roots.
   j) Training for parochial ministry inadequate.
   k) Unfair system of preferment and promotion.
   l) Inadequate stipend for level of responsibility.

2. MINISTERIAL AND PAROCHIAL
   a) Too much time spent on administration.
   b) Multi-parish benefices inhibit pastoral ministry
      by duplication of effort and repetition.
   c) Pastoral reorganisation counter-productive.
   d) Fund-raising for essential repair work to ancient
      fabric is a drain on local resources.
   e) Competing priorities.
   f) Diminishing lay appreciation and support.
   g) Conflicting expectations – lay/hierarchical.
   h) Inflexibility of parochial system.

3. PERSONAL
   a) Ill-health
   b) Tied accommodation
   c) Dual Career conflict
   d) Work/Family conflict.
   e) Clerical isolation.
   f) Moonlighting (taking on additional paid work to
      make ends meet).

ACTION ONE: DEALING WITH CAUSES

1. List the main stressors in your life
2. Which of these are self inflicted or avoidable?
3. Decide what you can do to reduce or discard self inflicted or avoidable stress
4. **DO IT.**
5. Analyse each unavoidable stressor. Break each one down into its constituent parts (eg. what exactly is causing you stress?)
6. Decide what you can do to reduce unavoidable stress

A trusted friend or colleague may be very useful in helping you decide which stressors are self-inflicted or avoidable. Others may be able to help you analyse unavoidable stressors, but you may need help from a counsellor to do this

ACTION TWO: SUPPORT

People who receive adequate physical, emotional, and psychological support are less vulnerable to pressure and are less likely to suffer the effects of stress.

If the level of support you receive at work or at home is low then ask for and be prepared to accept support from:

AT WORK –

Colleagues
Churchwardens/P.C.C.
Archdeacon/Rural Dean
Self-help groups, e.g. A.A.

AT HOME -

Spouse
Family
Friends
Help agencies, e.g. Marriage Guidance

DO IT EARLY

DO IT NOW

Measure of Support

1 = very strongly disagree
2 = strongly disagree
3 = disagree
4 = agree
5 = strongly agree
6 = very strongly agree

At Work

1. I have sufficient training to do my job   1 2 3 4 5 6
2. My Bishop is supportive and encouraging   1 2 3 4 5 6
3. I get plenty of feedback from my Bishop   1 2 3 4 5 6
4. My deanery colleagues are supportive   1 2 3 4 5 6

5. The Churchwardens/PCC are loyal   1 2 3 4 5 6
6. There is a good communication system   1 2 3 4 5 6

At Home

1. My partner is very supportive   1 2 3 4 5 6
2. My family is very supportive   1 2 3 4 5 6
3. I get practical support from friends   1 2 3 4 5 6
4. My GP is likely to be helpful should I
    become ill   1 2 3 4 5 6
5. I know someone who will help/listen
    to me when needed   1 2 3 4 5 6
6. I do not feel isolated   1 2 3 4 5 6

High scores mean you are getting good support at work/
home. Low scores mean you are getting a low level of support.

ACTION THREE: EXERCISE IS GOOD FOR YOU

Swimming, cycling, jogging, and other forms of physical activity are excellent ways of releasing tension caused by the stresses of everyday living. The feeling of tiredness brought on by physical effort helps to promote deep and refreshing sleep. The survival skills of the past, running, jumping, lifting, dragging, and climbing, evolved over millions of years to promote the hunting and gathering of food, are used less and less in today's high-tech society, and the human body is thus deprived of a major source of regeneration and self-healing.

- Exercise stimulates the body's own natural maintenance and repair system
- It strengthens the body's defences against infection by releasing protein from the muscles and preventing the build up of stress inducing steroids including cortisone.
- It improves respiration by relaxing the diaphragm and activating the lungs, thereby increasing the amount of oxygen in the blood
- It releases stored adrenalin (which is associated with increased aggression).
- It improves the staying power of the heart and circulation and may protect against coronary heart disease.
- It makes you feel good, in mind as well as body.

ACTION FOUR: EAT WELL AND STAY WELL

Keeping yourself physically fit and active is reinforced by ensuring that you and your body are getting the right kind of nourishment. The average person takes in about half-a-ton of food a year, as well as an equally staggering amount of drink. Although our bodies are extremely efficient at extracting just what it needs from this enormous intake, it can only cope up to a point. If you go on eating and drinking too much of some things and not enough of others, you will soon get out of condition, and your health and well-being will suffer. Ask yourself this question, 'How much good is what I am eating really doing me ?'

What you eat and the way it affects your body is dependent on a number of factors, including the genes you inherit from your parents which can determine how your body metabolism reacts to and copes with particular foods, and also the tendency to put on weight rather easily, which often runs in families. Your parents may also have shaped your own eating habits and attitudes to food such as a likeness for sweet things, snacking between meals, and having 'chips' with everything !

How much time and money you spend on food, how much alcohol you drink and how much exercise you take, can alter the balance between food and fitness, particularly when it comes to calories.

(Age and sex may affect this balance for the older we get the more likely we are to put on weight. This is especially so for women).

Almost everything we eat contains energy measured as calories: the higher the calorie rating, the more energy. But we should beware of thinking that eating extra rich energy foods will make us more energetic ! The amount of energy in our daily diet should exactly balance the energy our body burns up. If we eat more than we use, the surplus energy is stored as body fat.

If we are overweight the disadvantages range from difficulty in choosing clothes to fit, difficulty in getting about, awkwardness, embarrassment, and even marital disharmony, to more serious problems like shortness of breath, varicose veins, foot trouble, backache, arthritis, chest trouble, gallstones, high blood pressure, diabetes, heart attack and stroke.

Overweight people are also more likely to be accident victims, to have difficulty in pregnancy, and to suffer complications after an operation.

Body Image

Body image refers to the mental picture that a person has of their own body. People with anorexia nervosa tend to have a very negative body image; they sometimes feel that their body, or part of their body, is very much fatter than it really is. It is not unusual to mistake strong feelings for facts which is a thinking error (see below), e.g. I feel fat, therefore I must be fat. The way that someone feels about their body is often a reflection of how they view themselves as a person. Having a negative or distorted body image, therefore may seriously undermine an individual's self-confidence. People tend to feel worse about their bodies when they are feeling low and helpless in general. The problem with transferring feelings about yourself onto your body is that it results in a vicious cycle; losing weight and trying to change your body does not really solve the problem as the underlying issues remain unsolved.

HEALTH HABIT CHECK-LIST

1.	Air	[ ]	I do not smoke
2.	Water	[ ]	I seldom or never have more than four alcoholic drinks per sitting.
3.	Food	[ ]	I eat a substantial breakfast every day or almost every day.
4.	Exercise	[ ]	I take long walks or engage in sport swimming, gardening, or other physical activity at least 3 times a week.
5.	Rest	[ ]	I regularly have 7 – 8 hours of sleep.
6.	Regularity	[ ]	I seldom or never eat between meals.
7.	Moderation	159	

Health Status Ages for men and women

AGE	0-2 HABITS	3 HABITS	4 HABITS	5 HABITS	6 HABITS	7 HABITS
20-24	+14.3	+ 7.4	+ 0.5	- 1.1	- 4.2	- 9.4
25-29	+15.6	+ 8.3	+ 1.8	- 0.9	- 4.5	-10.2
30-34	+16.9	+ 9.1	+ 3.0	- 0.6	- 4.7	-11.1
35-39	+18.2	+ 9.9	+ 4.2	- 0.4	- 5.0	-12.0
40-44	+19.4	+10.7	+ 5.4	- 0.1	- 5.2	-12.9
45-49	+20.7	+11.6	+ 6.7	+ 0.1	- 5.5	-13.8
50-54	+22.0	+12.4	+ 7.9	+ 0.3	- 5.7	-14.7
55-59	+23.3	+13.2	+ 9.1	+ 0.6	- 6.0	-15.5
60-64	+24.5	+14.0	+10.4	+ 0.8	- 6.2	-16.4
65-69	+25.8	+14.8	+11.6	+ 1.1	- 6.5	-17.3
70-74	+27.1	+15.7	+12.8	+ 1.3	- 6.8	-18.2

A Healthy life style promotes both quality and length of life.

ACTION FIVE: GET FIT AND STAY FIT

EXERCISE – THE BEST TRANQUILLISER
If healthy, start slowly, work up to 30 – 40 minutes brisk exercise 3 to 4 times a week. You should get a little out of breath when exercising.
If in doubt, consult your doctor first.

WATCH YOUR WEIGHT
A strategy is better than a diet. If overweight, lose a little slowly by **Eating Less.**

EAT WISELY
Avoid sweet things, added salt, **LESS** fat, especially animal fat, **LESS** dairy foods, **MORE** fish, chicken, vegetables, fruit, bran.

ALCOHOL
A little – at times of relaxation – is good for you
BEWARE OF ADDICTION !

SMOKING
DON'T
IF YOU DO – SEEK HELP IN STOPPING

REGULAR CHECK-UPS
Blood pressure, cholesterol level, cervical smears and mammogram.

CHECK LIST
1. I get enough proper exercise	yes/no
2. My diet is healthy	yes/no

If the answers to the above questions are **NO**
What do you intend to do about it ?

3. I am overweight	yes/no
4. I drink too much alcohol	yes/no
5. I smoke	yes/no
6. I should be having a health check	yes/no

If the answers to the above questions are **YES**
what do you intend to do about it ?

ACTION SIX – LIFESTYLE

Getting enough –

SLEEP – average 8 hours
REST and RELAXATION
DAYS OFF and HOLIDAYS
TIME for LEISURE ACTIVITIES

Using time efficiently

Discontinue low priority activities
Delegate whenever possible
Do things more efficiently

Planning your time

Have time for the important not just the urgent
Decide priorities
Do things one at a time

Remember – failing to plan is planning to fail

CHECK LIST

DO I GET ENOUGH –

SLEEP ?
REST AND RELAXATION ?
DAYS OFF AND HOLIDAYS ?
LEISURE TIME ?

If the answer is NO to any of the above
What do you intend to do about it ?

....
....
....
....
....

DO I -

 USE TIME EFFICIENTLY ?
 PLAN MY TIME WELL ?
 DO THINGS ONE AT A TIME ?

If the answer is NO to any of the above,
What do you intend to do about it ?

....
....
....
....
....

ACTION SEVEN – LIFE PRIORITIES

Experience shows that failing to give time and energy to the things which we believe to be most important to us, often results in stress.

MAKE SURE THAT YOUR OVERALL LIFE PRIORITIES HAVE BEEN SET BY YOU AND NOT BY CIRCUM-STANCES
- AND KEEP THEM UNDER REVIEW.

OVERALL PRIORITIES

My overall priorities are:
(from 1 to 8 in column A)

Column A	Column B
1...............................	1...............................
2...............................	2...............................
3...............................	3...............................
4...............................	4...............................
5...............................	5...............................
6...............................	6...............................
7...............................	7...............................
8...............................	8...............................

Now go back and put a number from one to eight in column B in the order that you are actually giving them.

If the numbers on the right and on the left are not the same – what do you intend to do ?

....
....
....

The priorities of life are usually **Family** centred and then **Work** centred.

ACTION EIGHT – WHAT TYPE OF PERSON ARE YOU?

Casual about appointments	1 2 3 4 5 6 7	Never late
Not competitive	1 2 3 4 5 6 7	Very competitive
Good listener	1 2 3 4 5 6 7	Anticipate what others are going to say (nod, try to finish for them)
Never feel rushed (even under pressure)	1 2 3 4 5 6 7	Always rushed
Can wait patiently	1 2 3 4 5 6 7	Impatient while waiting
Take things one at a time	1 2 3 4 5 6 7	Try to do many things at once, thinks about what to do next
Care about satisfying yourself no matter what others think	1 2 3 4 5 6 7	Want a good job recognised by others
Slow doing things	1 2 3 4 5 6 7	Fast doing things
Easy going	1 2 3 4 5 6 7	Hard driving
Express feelings	1 2 3 4 5 6 7	Hide feelings
Many outside interests	1 2 3 4 5 6 7	Few interests outside work/home
Unambitious	1 2 3 4 5 6 7	Ambitious
Casual	1 2 3 4 5 6 7	Eager to get things done

High scores mean you have Type A behaviour
Low scores mean you have Type B behaviour

Some Type A's are known as AHA Types – Angry, Hostile, Aggressive.

Type A's live in the fast lane, are often workaholics, welcome change, and are almost addicted to 'adrenalin'.

Type B's are more laid back, and more philosophical.
Type A's after prolonged, often self-imposed pressures, may develop high blood pressure, heart attacks, strokes.

If you are a TYPE A person study the following hints:

- Slow down
- Accept the things you cannot change
- Do one thing at a time
- Smile
- Listen more, talk less
- Enjoy delays
- Make use of your 'spare' time by:
  reading
  listening to music
  enjoying the scenery
  switching off
- Do not take on more than you can handle

Maslow's* hierarchy of needs/drives presents us with a view of human motivation. The most urgent drives are the physiological, which includes hunger and thirst. As this level of drive is fulfilled, the safety drives begin to express themselves. Beyond the safety drives are drives for love, then the drives for esteem, and ultimately the drives for self-actualisation. Each person is at some level in the hierarchy.

Every one has crucial needs for:-

love and security
significance
worth or value

*Maslow, A.H. (1970) Motivation and Personality (2nd Ed.) New York: Harper & Row

When these are threatened, stress may be the outcome. People who receive their basic needs from entirely dependable sources are less vulnerable to stress.

I get my love and security from:

....
....
....

I get my significance, worth, value from:-

....
....
....

ACTION NINE – OBJECTIVES IN LIFE

Think about and write down your objectives for:-

Your work ....

Your spouse ....

Your children ....

Your finances ....

Yourself ....

Can I achieve these objectives?

Are these objectives realistic?

PERCEPTIONS

The degree of distress caused by an unpleasant or uncomfortable event at work or at home (a stressor) is related to how we think and feel about it. Remember, it is not a pressure or an event or a circumstance which determines whether you will suffer from stress, but your belief, thinking and attitude about it.

Do you worry too much ?   yes-no
Do you usually expect the worse?   yes-no

If the answer is yes to either or both, ask yourself -
What is really upsetting me ?
Is my thinking about it -
rational ?
exaggerated ?
wrong ?
flawed in any way ?
Are there other (less pessimistic) ways of thinking about it ?
Change your thinking so that it becomes
more rational
less exaggerated
more realistic
less pessimistic

THINKING ERRORS

a) *All or nothing thinking*. This is where things are seen only as black or white and there are no shades of grey. One mistake leads to total failure.

b) *Overgeneralisation*. Here one unfortunate event leads to the assumption that this will happen every time, but remember there is no justification for seeing one instance as proving the rule.

c) *Mental filter*. This is where you pick out and dwell exclusively on the negative or worrying details.

d) *Disqualifying the positive*. Here positive experiences do not count for some reason. Successes are a 'fluke'. No pleasure is taken from positive events.

e) *Jumping to conclusions*. You may assume the worst when there is no reason to, e.g. expecting failure before having tried.

f) *Catastrophising*. Here you exaggerate your own imperfections, e.g. 'I made a mistake, how awful, I can never show my face here again'. Common misfortunes become disasters. Do you think about other people's mistakes in the same way?

g) *Emotional reasoning*. This means taking your feelings as facts, e.g. because you feel so afraid, there must really be some danger.

h) *'Should' statements*. Thinking you should be able to stay calm all the time or you should never get angry. Rigid statements like this are overdemanding and unreasonable, and cause unnecessary pressure.

i) *Labelling and mislabelling*. You label yourself as a 'useless person' on the basis of one mistake. It makes as much sense as labelling yourself as a joiner because you put up a shelf.

j) *Personalisation*. Everything that goes wrong you attribute to yourself.

RIGHT THINKING

The aim of cognitive therapy is to help you to think in a more positive way and enable you to cope with the stresses and strains of life more easily.

STEP ONE: Learning to recognise the symptoms

Negative thoughts are automatic – they just seem to happen without any basis of reason or logic. They are our own inter-pretation of what is going on around us rather than facts.

Negative thoughts depend on how we feel at the time, our level of self-confidence, and what is happening in our lives. If we feel confident and happy, then the automatic thoughts we have are likely to reflect this by being positive and optimistic. If we unhappy and low in confidence our thinking is likely to be negative and pessimistic.

The negative thoughts we have about ourselves rarely coin-cide with reality; and, even if they are not actually irrational, they make us feel worse and can prevent us from feeling better. Because they are automatic we are unable to stand back from them and evaluate or question them.

STEP TWO: Putting thoughts to paper

If you start to feel bad about yourself and about what is happening to you, review your thoughts by putting them down on paper, perhaps in a diary. Try to correct your thinking by answering each of the negative statements you make about yourself with a more positive and balanced outlook.

Try to generate as many more reasonable alternatives to the negative thinking as possible. For example, instead of thinking 'I'll never get this done', or, 'I'm a failure at everything I do', you might think, 'I've got this far, so I cannot be a failure; and, anyway, I am learning to cope much better by under-standing more what's happening to me'.

Although a negative thought may not actually be wrong, the fact that it makes you feel bad is a good reason for trying to think more positively.

LOOKING FOR RATIONAL ANSWERS

1) **What is the evidence?**
    What evidence do I have to support my thoughts? What evidence do I have against them?
2) **What alternative views are there?**
    How would someone else view this situation? How would

I have viewed it before I got depressed? What evidence do I have to back these alternatives?

3) **What is the effect of thinking the way I do?**
Does it help me, or hinder me from getting what I want? What would be the effect of looking at things less negatively?

4) **What thinking error am I making?**
Am I thinking in all-or-nothing terms? Am I condemning myself as a total person on the basis of a single event?

Am I concentrating on my weaknesses and forgetting my strengths?

Am I blaming myself for something which is not my fault?

Am I taking something personally which has little or nothing to do with me?

Am I expecting myself to be perfect?

Am I using a double standard – how would I view someone else in my situation?

Am I paying attention only to the black side of things? Am I overestimating the chances of disaster? Am I exaggerating the importance of events?

Am I fretting about the way things ought to be instead of accepting and dealing with them as they come?

Am I assuming I can do nothing to change my situation?

Am I predicting the future instead of experimenting with it?

ACTION TEN – ASSERTIVENESS

Are you assertive enough ?

Remember – People frequently take us at our own value!
Below is a check list to help you to determine your level of
assertiveness.

- Fear of unpleasant consequences from being too assertive
  (anxious about saying 'No', afraid of an argument).
- Perceiving situations or other people as threatening (being
  unsure of your ability, adopting a low profile).
- Failing to think rationally about yourself (frequently
  comparing yourself unfavourably to other people).
- Confusing assertion and aggression (being unduly deferen-
  tial and apologetic to avoid being seen as aggressive).
- Failing to develop assertive skills (being encouraged to
  behave unassertively).
- Equating non-assertiveness with politeness (keeping quiet
  rather than disagree with someone else).
- Confusing non-assertiveness with helpfulness (not always
  helpful, and the reverse may be true).

Clergy find it particularly difficult to be assertive. The reasons
for this are as much to do with cultural conditioning as to
personality. A degree of assertiveness is positively beneficial,
however, in establishing the right kind of authority to make
things happen and to get things done

The right kind of assertiveness at meetings:

Keep your own contributions short and to the point
Avoid interrupting others
Do not let others interrupt you
Do not wait until the last moment to make your own
contribution
Use eye contact (but non-threateningly)
Use appropriate body language !

At the appropriate opportunity, practice your assertiveness
skills by:

1. *Standing up for your rights:*
   Making complaints
   Learning when to say NO
   Voicing your opinion
   Refusing to be put down

2. *Expressing positive feelings*
   Telling someone you appreciate them
   Giving due praise
   Receiving praise without embarrassment
   Initiating conversation

3. *Expressing negative feelings:*
   Showing that you are hurt
   Showing that you are angry

Your acquired counselling and care skills (see above) will enable you to judge when it is appropriate to be assertive, and also when it is highly inappropriate.

ACTION ELEVEN: RELAXATION TRAINING

1) Relaxation is a skill which has to be learned (or relearned).
2) Learning involves practice. In order to learn relaxation techniques properly you need to set aside at least 20 minutes per day to go through the exercises.
3) If you do not make this commitment to set aside this time on a daily basis, you will not benefit from relaxation training.
4) You need to practice the relaxation exercises in a quiet room alone where you will not be disturbed.
5) Either lie on a bed, on the floor, or sit in a comfortable armchair.
6) Loosen any tight clothing, such as a belt or clerical collar, and preferably take off your shoes.
7) Make sure that you are in a comfortable state, ie not too hot or cold, before you begin.
8) Set your own pace.
9) Remember to concentrate on breathing slowly, smoothly and evenly, and not too deeply throughout the exercises.
10) Relaxation training should only take place when there is no time pressure, eg practice should *not* take place 15 minutes before you are due to leave to take a service or make a pastoral call.
11) As daily practice is *crucial*, set aside a regular time each day for your relaxation exercises, eg after pastoral work, after your evening meal, or just before going to bed. Do *not* just use relaxation when you feel a bit anxious.
12) Once you learn to relax and are comfortable with the relaxation exercises, you will be in a position to combat anxiety in 'real life' situations.

ACTION TWELVE: RELAXATION EXERCISE

Sit well back in the chair so that your back is supported. Place a small cushion in the small of your back if this is more comfortable.

Move the legs forward so that the whole of the weight of the upper leg is supported.

Allow your knees to roll outwards a little.

Make sure that your buttock muscles are soft and spreading, and that your abdomen is loose and soft so that your breathing is not constrained.

Think of your shoulders dropping down towards your waist so that you feel more space between your neck and shoulders.

Make sure that your elbows are not pressed into your sides, and let your hands rest on your thighs. Your hands should not be touching.

Your head should be perfectly balanced at the top of your spine – not leaning back, or to one side.

Close your eyes lightly, if appropriate. If not, focus your gaze on a non-moving object.

Let your body sink into the chair and enjoy the feeling.

Listen to the sounds around you with interest; with your mind's eye, picture a favourite place – perhaps a holiday in the sun, or an idyllic day out.

Just sit as long as you want to. You may feel fidgety at first, but persevere with the practice. You will find that in time you will be able to sit quietly for longer periods.

Remember, relaxation is not a waste of time. It allows the body, mind, and spirit, to re-energise and recuperate, especially after periods of high arousal, anxiety, and stress.

POSTSCRIPT

Of all the coping mechanisms which are available to those who are called to serve in Our Lord's sacred ministry, the most powerful is that of prayer. Prayer is not just about asking God to do something. This has been done already in the saving grace of His Son, Jesus Christ; it is also about allowing ourselves to believe in His grace to the point where we are able to accept His healing and forgiveness. We cannot so easily accept forgiveness of ourselves for the wrong we attribute to our own shortcomings. BUT HE CAN; AND HE HAS.